CONVICTIONS

CONVICTIONS

My Journey from the Convent to the Courtroom

ARLENE VIOLET

with

SUDA J. PROHASKA

RANDOM HOUSE
NEW YORK

Library of Congress Cataloging-in-Publication Data

Violet, Arlene.
Convictions.

1. Violet, Arlene. 2. Attorneys-general—Rhode
Island—Biography. 3. Ex-nuns—Rhode Island—Biography.
I. Prohaska, Suda J., 1945-   . II. Title.
KF373.V56A3 1987   353.97455 [B] 86-29646
ISBN 0-394-55182-6

Manufactured in the United States of America
23456789

To my mom, who taught me the lesson of the high wire.
Why walk across it when you can dance?

The events in this book are true. Except for public figures, or private persons whose matters are of public record, the names of people, where appropriate, have been changed to protect their privacy.

CONTENTS

CONVICTIONS

PROLOGUE

When I was a child growing up, I never dreamed that I would become a nun. I thought I would get married like everybody else and raise kids. I was headed for that, but life intervened. I found myself going against my family's wishes and becoming a woman of the cloth, leaving behind the man I loved.

When I was a nun, I never dreamed that I would take on bishops and march in protests. I always thought you were on their side and they were on yours. I never thought that living in housing projects for fifteen years would show me the difference: the ghetto Christ from the paper Church.

I never dreamed that when I was a young nun I would take on hoodlums and City Hall. Or that I would become a lawyer and be nicknamed "Attila the Nun." I never thought that I would sue a bishop and face excommunication.

After twenty-three years of doing what I loved most, being a nun, I never dreamed that I would have to leave it all behind when I ran for public office. Or that I would eventually be elected this country's first woman state attorney general.

When I was attorney general, I never dreamed that I would retry Claus von Bülow, sit in a cell with a mobster, fight with politicians to rid the state of corrupt business practices, be profiled by *60 Minutes,* and employ bodyguards around the clock. Or that I would prosecute priests and police.

I never dreamed. I just followed my convictions. Sometimes they took you places you didn't want to go. But if you believed in your convictions, you couldn't help but get there.

1
BASEBALLS AND BATHTUBS

Back then, I couldn't make up my mind if I wanted to be a nun or a cop. Eventually I got to be both.

It's no accident that you usually have to pass by the men's room first on the way to the ladies' room. There's a rich symbolism here. Somehow, in the order of things, men got to go first, were considered first, and usually ended up first. Being a woman, nun, and lawyer was definitely breaking new ground if not old rules. You did not get to go first, were not considered first, and certainly, in the solidly male bastion of entrenched power in the Holy Roman Catholic Church, did not end up first.

But being first is not what's at issue here. Change is. Fundamentally and importantly, and there is a simple explanation for that in what is an otherwise all-too-complicated world. It has to do with growing up, first and lasting impressions, and, above all, deepening convictions.

Take growing up, for instance.

It was a different Providence then. In fact, the big gray three-decker tenement at 216 Plain Street, where I lived with my parents, brother, and sister, has been torn down and replaced by a medical center. In the real estate version of life, there is no death, just the constantly changing pattern of sod and concrete.

But when I was growing up, our street looked like the main

street in Sinclair Lewis's novel of the same name. Our house was square dab in the middle of just about everything. There were other tenement houses, to be sure, but there were also a number of businesses. At one end of the street were Manny's meat market and general store, an icehouse, and Rhode Island Hospital. Down our block the other way were a bakery and Louie's variety store.

Back then, Plain Street was a blue-collar neighborhood all the way: multiethnic, tight-knit, proud, and heavily Catholic. The kind of Catholic that was firmly bound to Sunday attendance at church and the traditional observances of the faith. Mass, for example, was very important. Going to church was a visible sign that you were in good graces with Somebody, or at least trying to be. When you didn't have much, that meant a lot. It was also comforting to your neighbor. While perception may have been everything to some who kept score of those things, to most in that parish it was just a nice feeling to be there at worship with your family and friends.

The nuns, in particular, were especially appealing to me: They lived their lives helping others. They served people who were proud and independent, for the most part, who disliked owing anyone money. So they didn't.

My dad was a lot like that, too.

He was French–Canadian and Irish, an uncanny businessman, and a caring father. He had that kind of natural built-in warmth that made you feel like there was a great big furnace stoked up inside him all the time, and it made you want to draw close. His name was Henry, but everyone called him Mickey. He wasn't very tall, just about five feet nine, but he was chunky and powerful. He loved his children and his wife, and we loved him.

My dad knew how to save a dollar but he knew how to spend one, too. On the saving side, he owned the triple-decker in which we lived. He rented out the other two floors to pay the mort-

gage. He had his eye on a gas station next door, so he took out
a lease. After putting in eighteen-hour days, and when it made
enough money, he bought it, just like that. Then he convinced
a friend of his to go partners with him on buying some property
for parking lots. They bought one, made some money, then
bought another one. One step at a time. The value of hard work,
particularly his, impressed me enormously as a child.

On the spending side, my dad was a generous man. It was not
unusual to see him walk down the street, cigar clenched between
his teeth, with a tip of the hand to the forehead when he met
passersby. On occasion, somebody who was down on his or her
luck would approach him. Once when an old widow asked him
for help, I saw him without any hesitation reach deep into his
pocket and retrieve a twenty-dollar bill. He pressed it into her
hand with a delighted smile on his face, and after a few words
of encouragement continued on his way. My dad was well respected by the neighborhood. His charity was renowned. I never
forgot what I saw.

These acts of generosity didn't seemed to fluster my mother,
Alice. She accepted his way of life because he was her life. She
was always fussing over him, trying to make things just so in
order to please him. It didn't take much; he didn't require a great
deal even though my mom had a great deal to give. We children
were the lucky ones; we got all the overflow. She was the quintes-
sential homemaker, so we were constantly the centers of attention. When you're young, you expect that. When you're older,
you appreciate it.

Mom was also a knockout with her enormous brown eyes and
flapper-style hairdo. Bette Davis paled by comparison, even
though it is Bette Davis to whom my mother is often compared.
But she also had such a gentleness about her that it could coax
you right out of any bad mood in which you might find yourself.
Real or imagined. She has special gifts of the heart that just seem
to multiply with age.

Even in her seventies, my mom is lovely. But she has finally taken the slipcovers off her furniture. Years ago, she had to keep everything covered because my brother, sister, and I constantly roughhoused. Well, two of us roughhoused. Alice Ann, who is five years older than I, was a perfect lady. She didn't play cowboys, and she didn't play Indians, but she sure knew how to play dolls. She even dressed like one.

If Alice Ann set the temperature of what to expect in a child, then my thermometer must have been broken. I was scrawny, possessed a mass of jet-black hair that was in a constant tangle of curls, and had a face that looked as if it had spent its entire career plastered in dirt. When you were busy stealing bases in sandlot baseball, or throwing a football for a nine-yard touchdown in somebody's backyard, being the Ivory soap girl was not a real big priority. I seemed to love dirt. I know I loved to play in it, and the dirtier I could get, the happier I was. My mom always said I was a very happy child.

But the hair bothered me to no end. It was always in the way of my blue-gray eyes and I jabbed at it constantly, grimy fingers and all, to knock it back. I finally got my hair chopped off in a pixie in high school, a variation of which I wear today. I was a little independent kid then and more or less stayed that way. In constant motion and in constant trouble.

Alice Ann had a campaign. She hoped and prayed that I would eventually be sent to charm school to get my priorities straightened out.

"Arlene, dear," she cooed, "I think you would love Elmhurst Academy. They could do so many wonderful things for you. You'll thank me later."

Elmhurst was run by the Madames of the Sacred Heart. They wanted you to act grown up and dignified. I just wanted to swing from trees and play kick-the-can. I never went.

My sister and I get together every so often to talk about these experiences growing up. They include our brother. Although he is nearly four years older than me, we looked and acted a lot alike.

I think that one of the reasons we got along so well, besides our love of sports, was the fact that we both did so poorly in school. No matter how badly Buddy did, he was comforted by the knowledge that I did worse.

My parents never saw my report card first. Buddy did. I remember one time when he pulled me down by the hand to the seat next to his to compare, and meticulously counted up the number of D's, E's, or F's I had. I could sense his growing excitement when he counted more.

"Look at this, Arlene," he shrieked. "How could you get so many?" as if he never had any. He broke into chortles of laughter and slapped his knees in delight with the palm of his hand. I laughed, too, because I liked him so much. He was my big brother, after all. When we compared grades the next time, he had more failing marks than I. But Buddy wasn't disheartened; all that meant was that we just matched. As a result both of us came out feeling pretty good.

Getting me to go to school was like pulling teeth. I couldn't stand the thought of being cooped up all day. My dad had to teach me some lessons of his own. They eventually worked.

"Arlene," he said to me, smiling, "how would you like to have this nice fifty-cent piece?" In 1949, that was a huge sum of money.

I looked up at him to make sure that was what he held in his hand. Sure enough, it was. "What do I have to do to get that?" I asked.

"Oh," he said, flipping the coin into the air a few times to make sure he had my attention, "I guess you would have to go back to school and stay there until it was time for you to come back here." Then he winked at me. "Pretty, isn't it?"

I felt like one of those big black crows that like shiny objects. I couldn't keep my eyes off the coin, or my hands. "You've got yourself a deal, Dad.'' It worked every time. He never tired of it and neither did I. I was getting rich.

However, it took more than money to give me brains. If it hadn't been for my sister, I don't know what would have happened to me. There had been a theory at the time that brains were hereditary. My sister was very, very smart. Somebody figured out that I would eventually grow into mine. In truth my real problem was poor eyesight. I needed glasses, couldn't see a thing, but hated the thought of having to wear them. I never told anybody. What I couldn't see, I memorized. But one morning I made a fatal mistake. I brushed a breakfast cereal raisin off the table, thinking it was a fly. My mom marched me straight down to the eye doctor. Now glasses are so much a part of my face, I don't think anybody would recognize me without them. When you're young, you're lost with them. When you're older, you're lost without them.

Wearing them, however, did not improve my handwriting. I am left-handed, but the nuns tried to make me write with my right hand. That really gummed up the works. On those days when I felt particularly frustrated, I couldn't wait to get out of school to devote myself to something important, like play.

You either played the good guy or the bad guy. I always wanted to be the good guy, somebody I admired, like a nun or a policeman. Once I imagined that I was a great sleuth in pursuit of a shady desperado. I didn't just peer around a corner, hoping to spot my little playmate. I actually tried to recall every detail about my friend. Was he athletic? Did he climb trees? Or would he hide in a trash can because he was clever and small and knew I didn't like bad smells? I analyzed everything about that person and tried to think as he thought.

I was sharpening skills that I relied upon later. Only I didn't know that then. How we play at life as children is often how we live it as adults. Back then, I couldn't make up my mind if I wanted to be a nun or a cop. Eventually I got to be both.

When I wasn't playing, I tagged around with my dad at the gas station. I never got near the pumps: My father was afraid I would get run over. I stood back at a distance and watched him.

My dad liked his community. He was the kind of man who put more into it than he got out of it. He was happy knowing that someone or some group was going to be a little better off as a result of his efforts. He worked for a strong sports program to keep the youth off the streets and out of trouble. When the Republicans looked around for someone who could be a successful candidate on their ticket, they approached him. They liked his style and ability.

In return my dad liked what politics was supposed to be able to do. He saw it as a real opportunity to serve people. He accepted the Republican party's overtures and ran for alderman in a completely Democratic city, Providence. He won office. People, despite their party affiliation, recognized that my father would work for their needs, not his. He proved them right.

Governor William Vanderbilt, also a Republican, was initially interested in my dad's blue-collar connections and the blue-collar vote. He thought my dad could help. My dad could and did. Governor Vanderbilt saw in my father someone who was honest and sincere and, equally important, someone who knew and understood people. A strong friendship developed between the two when my dad became Vanderbilt's campaign manager.

My dad was a little older, certainly a little stockier, and infinitely poorer, but both men shared a love of people. And that was the bond that sparked their friendship. I can't say for sure that Vanderbilt was as comfortable in blue-collar circles as my father was among Vanderbilt's peers. But it didn't seem to make a whole lot of difference to them, or their families. They just liked each other.

My mom and Ann Vanderbilt got along well, too. I hung around the kitchen when my mom cooked dinner for the four of them, trying to get a little extra scoop of something good, and asking her what she thought. Mostly, she was worried about anything being good. She was not a great cook, knew it, and went into a panic every time my dad suggested that the Vanderbilts come over for dinner. But she always had time for me.

"I think the Vanderbilts are some of the most down-to-earth people I've ever met," she said, as she nervously patted down a chicken that she was about to bake as if it had just stolen three thousand dollars and she was trying to find it. "I feel a little funny having them here because they're so wealthy and used to such fine things. Every time we go to their house, they have such elegant china and servants to take care of everything. But they don't seem to mind coming here, and your father thinks it's all right."

"Well, what do you think?" I asked slyly. I knew my mom didn't always want to tell you her innermost feelings.

"I like them, Arlene." She stopped what she was doing for a minute and looked at me. "You know, Ann is so thoughtful. You remember the other day she had sent us some beautiful flowers and I didn't have anything to put them in, so I put them in the bathtub for a while. Later, when Ann was in town, her driver brought her over for a visit and she noticed what I had done. She immediately ordered a gorgeous vase to put them in." My mother beamed at me, the fondness of the memory bringing her delight.

I could tell by the way that my mom and Mrs. Vanderbilt talked and laughed that they liked each other. My folks named my sister after Ann Vanderbilt.

Whenever my folks went to the Vanderbilts' house in Portsmouth for dinner, the Vanderbilts always put on their best for them. My parents were the salt of the earth as far as the Vanderbilts were concerned and they showed it literally. It was no coincidence that my parents were accorded their own salt and pepper shakers while taking supper. Vanderbilt custom demanded it, but not all the Vanderbilt guests got it. As a matter of fact, the Vanderbilts had put a premium on salt and pepper in those days. It had nothing to do with price, but everything to do with something called honesty.

It seems as though wealthy, titled, and impeccably well-educated friends of the Vanderbilts' were stealing their hosts' salt and pepper shakers. Their idea of Souvenir City, apparently, if not a desire to become the new movers and shakers in town. Another demonstration of who truly are the haves and have-nots in this world. In this instance my parents, who had not, had. And the Vanderbilts, who had, had not. But they knew whom they could trust in the future. And in that knowledge comes the real having.

2
REFLECTIONS

His death came as a double shock to me. When he died, so did my catechism.

The future is often precarious. What is yours one day is not the next. I found that out at age fourteen when my father died. I attended Tyler School in Providence and had gone to a science fair at Brown University. I wanted to stay out later so I called home. My cousin answered the phone. She told me to come home right away. Then Buddy got on the phone and told me that our dad had died.

I was stunned. I put the phone back on the hook and stared at it as if it had just bitten me. I could feel its poisonous venom take hold and the life flow out of my body. I raced home with my remaining strength.

"What happened, Buddy?" I wailed. "He seemed just fine this morning at breakfast."

Buddy's eyes were heavy with tears. "He went on his usual rounds at nine this evening to pick up the parking receipts," he mumbled. "He started home and then just collapsed. I guess he must have had a massive heart attack." His voice trailed off.

My dad was only fifty-seven years old. I looked around for my mother. She was in a corner of the living room, sobbing. My cousin had her arms around her. I knew I was going to have to be the strong one for both of us, particularly after my father's funeral. That was when the loneliness would set in.

When my sister and brother returned to school, that left mom and me.

"Ma," I said, rubbing my hands together as if trying to ignite the presence of my father, "you are my best friend, do you know that?" I clasped her straight, narrow shoulders and looked carefully at her. My eyes burned. I wanted their fire to catch her heart.

Tears spilled down her cheeks. "Arlene," she whispered, "you are my joy." And then she smiled. My mom has a smile that could set birds singing in the cold of winter. It was worth more to me than words. I knew then that everything was going to be all right.

"We'll survive," she said simply, bobbing her head up and down. We fell silent, retreating to our own quiet thoughts, but at the top of the list was each other.

You of course can never take people's place. That's why they are who they are and you are who you are. At the time I was not concerned with illusive philosophies, or sophomoric stabs at profundity. I just wanted to help my mom and, in the process, me.

Death is not an experience devoid of living remedies. Consequently, I learned a great deal about life. I learned what it takes to be strong, and that on occasion it's okay to be weak. For the first time I learned what real pain is. I also began to understand the meaning of irony, how unforgiving it can be, and its subsequent place in my own chosen journey.

The first irony was that my father was not supposed to die, and, in my catechism of persons and things remarkable, could not. His death came as a double shock to me. When he died, so did my catechism.

I began to suspect that life was a lot like a game of marbles. Somebody was always trying to knock you off. While there were lessons to be learned here, I began to look beyond the rim of the circle for greater meaning. Death taught you to do that. In that search I found the following: You recognized what in your stock-pile of perfectly cold round pieces of glass was most precious to you, you treated that piece differently from all the others, and you spared no amount of energy to ensure its victory on the game board.

I applied certain analogies to my newfound insights. Whatever talents I had I would spend time developing and using them well. The beginnings of a life in service to others had started to take hold in my heart. And second, I would not be diverted in using these talents. I would cultivate them, sharpen them, and ulti-mately refine them. Victory was not always attainable, but in the high-stakes battlefield of your approach to life versus theirs, it was worth trying for.

I thought about the nuns with whom I had come in contact. They were the most focused people I knew. They were generous and loving and had devoted their lives to helping others. I wanted to use my skills as they did.

However, life is often a two-way pull. While I was suffused with new meanings, I was also becoming a real handful for my mother. I was serious about school, serious about theater, and serious about boys. Not necessarily in that order, but close.

I put a lot of my energies into the theater, playing secondary and lead roles just as I was doing in real life. For an adolescent, this seemed the adult thing to do.

One of my favorite characters was that of Jo in *Little Women.* I identified with the struggles of a family and the questions of sensitivity it evoked. Playing a part was the ultimate challenge. It meant you had to reach outside yourself to grasp the nature of another. That was a very rich exercise. It forced you to expand your mind, much as I had learned to do when I was a child engrossed in play.

Then I met Bob Turner. He was a sophomore at Providence College and gorgeous. I liked him and he liked me. He wasn't tall, but his Pacific-blue eyes stirred more than swirling waters. He and other PC men had been imported to our school temporarily to help out with our stage production of *Oklahoma.*

"Hi," he said. It wasn't much, but it was enough. I felt engulfed by a simmering sea.

"Hi, yourself," I said. It was, as they say, the start of a beautiful friendship.

Although I felt a tide rising after meeting Bob, Jim Standon was my steady boyfriend. He was a dear friend, someone whose affection I treasured very much. But I soon found myself in a heartbreaking situation for all three of us. I eventually began to date Bob at the same time I was seeing Jim. Jim wanted to give me an engagement ring when I was seventeen. Bob had no idea that there was an engagement ring, much less somebody from whom to receive it.

When you're young, there are supposed to be all kinds of excuses for playing both ends toward the middle. Frankly, I can't think of any now and neither could I then. Hurting people is still hurting people no matter how old you are. Adults are supposed to know better, but many of us rarely do.

When I wasn't throwing myself into a relationship, I threw myself into acting. I was starved for the theater. I wanted to nurture my entire being on the cutting edge of a stage. I traveled to New York frequently to see as many plays as I could. If a career was a banquet, then acting was my main course.

"Arlene," my mother said every time I left for New York, "don't burn yourself out. You've got so much ahead of you. You race here, race there. Why don't you just stay home for a while, give yourself a rest?"

My mom was a very wise woman. I was not. "Oh, Ma!" I said. "I don't want to miss anything! There are some terrific plays in New York this weekend. And you always meet the most interesting people!" Then I smiled at her and waved gaily. "I'll take it easy next weekend." I felt like Scarlett O'Hara talking about her beloved Tara.

Time, of course, is relative. So is salvation. While it may have been near at hand for others, my classmates and I figured it wasn't even on the horizon for us. I tended to be a little head-strong. With my father gone, I was used to doing pretty much what I wanted. But my mother trusted me and I respected that trust. She really didn't have anything about which to worry. I can't say that about the girl at the elevator door, however.

I saw her when I was in New York attending the national invitational tournament game at Madison Square Garden be-tween Providence College and St. John's. If you missed a good play, you could always find an equally good event at the Garden. Either way, you didn't lose. At least, in those days I didn't think you did. I had met a dashing college senior there who had promptly asked me out. I couldn't resist, couldn't think why I should, and didn't. The rest, as they say, however, is not history. On the way to meeting Mr. Suave, I noticed a young woman my age swaying in front of the elevator on my floor of the hotel where I was staying. She not only had a hard time figuring out which arrow went up and which arrow went down, but also, in the great cosmos of things, just exactly why they did. She had been drinking. From the state of things, it seemed, quite steadily. She gave me a boozy look, tried to smile, and half fell back against the wall. She positioned her buttocks against the solid plaster and then pushed outward. It gave the impression of stand-ing.

"Are you all right?" I asked uncertainly. I unconsciously reached out for her. The pale green of the walls and brown of the hotel's shag carpet were not becoming colors for her. If I don't catch her, I thought, she'll be wearing the carpet.

She brightened up visibly when she saw me and produced what she thought was an enthusiastic hand wave. "Hi, there,"

she slurred. Her hand wave reminded me of the queen mother's
after she had just reviewed two hundred thousand of her royal
subjects. It was limp and hardly noticeable. "Are you going to
meet your boyfriend?" she inquired. "I'm going to meet one of
them, too. I can't remember his name, but I'm sure he'll remember mine." She clutched her stomach for a moment and gri-
maced. "Ah-h-h, I feel sort of sick. Don't worry, though." She
raised her other hand in protest. "This happens all the time. It
will go away in a minute." She was quiet for a second, then she
hiccuped and dropped her hand to her mouth. "See, what did
I tell you? And here's the elevator, too," she said, swinging
around and lurching into it. "Hey, you! Aren't you coming?"

I smiled and shook my head and walked back to my room. I
had just looked in the mirror and the image had stared back. I
felt shaken to the core.

"Arlene!" my friends said when I returned. "What are you
doing back so soon? Did he stand you up?"

"No," I said absently. "I stood him up." My friends encouraged me to go downstairs and meet him, but I brushed them off.
"Look, I don't want to meet him. Frankly, I think he's too old
for me, and too fast. To tell you the truth, I just want to stay in
tonight to do a little reflecting and collect my thoughts." They
gave me a puzzled look, shrugged their shoulders, and walked
out. I watched them disappear down the hall and shut the door
behind me. I leaned against it. The air slowly escaped from my
lungs. I had been going too fast, and the good-looking young
man I had met at the game was a reminder of that. I needed to
slow down.

I got out of the evening wear I had carefully selected for that
night and pulled on my pajamas. The rooms on either side were
quiet. I didn't even turn on the television. I began to do what
I hadn't done in a long time: meditate. I thought back upon my
life, my values, what was important to me and what was not. I
folded my hands in my lap and crossed my legs underneath me.

I thought about Martin Luther King and civil rights, hunger, poverty, and justice. The more I thought about issues that used to carry great weight with me, the more I saw that the only person who had placed limitations on my life was me. I felt God had given me some unique talents and gifts and that I should be using them for the good and glory of people. I loved people, and it slowly dawned on me that perhaps what I really wanted to do was devote my life to helping them.

Back then, when I was young, sitting in that chair, I knew that my life had carried a special mark upon it. I was, in a real sense, apart from the others. I played and laughed and sang, but deep inside, like pools of water catching the late-afternoon sun, a reflective process always rippled through me. Nobody knew this, not even my mother. I had been so good at camouflaging my interior life, with its feelings and insights, that I had fooled myself best of all. It took a girl at the elevator to bring it all back.

There was only one hitch to this newly rediscovered thinking. Actually, there were three: Bob, my mother, and the theater.

3
CONVICTIONS

*"My aunt warned me about you. She never told me what it was,
but I wish I had listened to her."*

I felt I really wanted to be a nun. The people who were truly
making a difference in the world were the nuns. They were
doers, not sayers. I admired them as an architect admires a beau-
tifully appointed and functionally well-designed building. The
eloquence is in the deed, not in the promise.

I liked the kind of nuns who broke away from afternoon
prayers at the convent to tend to the needs of the people around
them. I saw them shake down shopkeepers to help a poor widow
who had no money or friends. They prayed through action, not
by mouth. They had guts and conviction. They weren't defined
by rule or ritual. They were guided by love. I wondered if I
could be like them. When I finally did realize it in September of
my senior year, I sent in my application to join the Sisters of
Mercy. The following March, I went out to Mount St. Rita's
convent in Cumberland for my interview with the provincial. I
felt the rush of my experience four years earlier at the Narragansett retreat house, where I had gone for a glimpse of the interior
life. The grounds at St. Rita's were equally spectacular; you had
the sense that this was a special place. I was stirred by similar
special feelings. I was also nervous. After all, I had taken some
big steps.

"Child." Mother Mary Helena smiled at me. "I have heard
much about you from our nuns, but tell me in your own words

why you think you have a vocation, and why you want to enter this particular order."

"I want to serve God," I said simply, "because I want to help people. Being a Sister of Mercy is the best way I know how to do that."

"What about the theater?" she prodded. She knew about my love of the theater and its possibility as a career choice.

My eyes sparkled and I broke into a big smile. "No secrets here!" I laughed. "Yes," I replied, "I do love the theater. Being onstage makes my heart soar. But unlike the theater, I feel that the religious life will allow me to leap over tall buildings."

I looked out the window briefly and saw that ice was formed along the windowsill. I turned back to her. "Being an actress would have its moments. Bringing an audience to tears, laughter, and reflection. But I want to produce true passion in people. I want to stir their souls and ignite their spirit, not just their emotions. When the applause dies down and the curtain drops, I want something left standing there that burns deep and lasts a long time: their convictions."

Mother Mary Helena listened attentively. She stood up. Our interview was over. She smiled and embraced me. "You know our policy," she said. "We will be considering all the applicants to see if they're suitable, and we'll be informing those who are later."

I walked outside and felt the cold wind upon my face. It stung my eyes and my heart. I believed every word I had spoken in my interview; I felt destined for the convent, but since September my friendship with Bob had deepened immeasurably. Like a boat whose sail was unfurled before the wind, I didn't know in which direction I was being blown. I had to find my own course.

It's one thing to keep a secret, but when its own silence defeats its purpose, you have to make a decision. I was accepted by the Mercys that summer. After having wrestled with love and the convent, I knew that I had truly spoken with my soul in March.

I began sharing that decision with the people I loved the most. I was always a very private person. What you don't tell people, you can't be asked about. Consequently, I had never told my friends what I had been thinking. None of them knew that I would be entering the convent in the fall. Had they known, they would have been horrified. Who would play with them in New York if I shut myself up behind four walls?

I had already discussed the convent with my mom. I had known ahead of time that she wouldn't like it. We were so close and had relied upon each other so much after my father's death. My leaving would be a tremendous blow. Even though I would only be twenty minutes up the road, it would be like entering another dimension. We wouldn't be just miles apart, we would be worlds apart.

"Ma," I had said, putting my arm around her, "I want to be a nun."

My mother always had a fear that I would up and enter the convent someday. She saw it coming in the eighth grade when I went on that retreat in Narragansett. "Don't let those nuns get their hands on you," she had warned. Now tears welled up in her eyes at my words.

"Are you sure?" she asked, her hand reaching for mine. "You're such a fun-loving girl. I can't imagine you for a minute cooped up in a place where you couldn't laugh." Lines of concern drew around her eyes. "Arlene, I honestly don't think you'll be happy." She shook her head back and forth sadly. "I have misgivings about this."

I squeezed her earnestly, at the same time pumping up my own strength. "I know right as rain that this is best for me. I have to at least give it a shot." I gave her an encouraging smile.

She didn't like my decision, but my mom believes in letting her children live their own lives. "What about Bob and Jim?" she asked simply. She liked them and even though it is the goal of every Catholic mother to see her daughter happily married, she had always felt I was too young for marriage.

As tough as it had been telling my mom, it was even tougher telling Bob and Jim. Our lives intertwined. I felt very bad when I pushed gently back into Jim's hand the engagement ring he had so proudly and lovingly tried to present me. "I can't accept this," I said. "I will never forget our times together, but this isn't right for either of us. We've grown comfortable with each other because we've known each other for so long." I touched his hand, wanting to touch his heart the way he had touched mine. "Thank you for honoring me." And then I said hurriedly, the way you drink a second cup of coffee when you know you're already ten minutes late, "I'm going to enter the convent." I fairly swallowed the words.

Jim's eyes burned momentarily with hurt. He was crestfallen, but ultimately understanding. He gave me a warm hug and moved on with his life.

I tossed and turned over Bob. He had become my man of the moment, hour, day. How could I possibly experience such enormous love for this man and still want to enter the convent? There was a spirituality in those days that said if you even thought you had a vocation but did nothing about it, you would be condemned to hell. The prevailing theory was that you had an obligation to try it first, and if you didn't like it, or it didn't like you, then you could always get married. Providing, of course, that there was still somebody to marry.

Bob was everything I could want in a man. He was warm, nurturing, and devoted. It didn't hurt that he was also incredibly attractive. I was in terrible conflict. But I also knew me, what I wanted and needed out of life. Although we had never talked about marriage, it didn't seem to be the answer for me. It felt limiting, and I wanted to embrace the world. By this time I had also spoken in confidence to some of the nuns about my decision and application to enter. Some had been elated; some were skeptical.

"Arlene," said one of those who was a skeptic, "your intentions are admirable, but your gifts are questionable. Not that you're not unusually bright and can tackle life with such unbridled enthusiasm, but it's precisely that enthusiasm that concerns me. You're headstrong and you keep your own counsel, traits that don't become the religious life. If you are accepted, I don't think you will be able to withstand the obligation of the vows."

I was hurt and baffled because my intentions had been so good, and after spending a great deal of time praying about the issue, I really did feel that I had a genuine vocation. I was drawn to this life as iron is drawn to the magnet. I knew I could make it because it was made for me. I was undaunted. As the good sister had said, I kept my own counsel.

I had to face Bob. I didn't like confrontations, and I felt this had every potential of building into one. His aunt was one of the nuns who knew I wanted to enter, and had strongly recommended against it. She had been warning Bob not to get too sweet on me. He didn't know why and hadn't paid any attention to her.

He came over to my house one evening. We had made plans to go out. "Hi," he said in a strong, easy voice. He kissed me and held me close. My response was tentative, unlike me. He pulled back and looked closely at me. He was acutely sensitive and could immediately decipher even my most closed moods. Moods that I thought were engagingly open. "What's the matter?" he said teasingly. "Can't you make up your mind about where you want to go tonight?"

"Bob." I looked up at him, my eyes brooding. "I wish it were as simple as that. The movies would be great, but we've got to talk first."

"Sure," he said, swinging me around by the shoulder and propelling me toward the front door as if my body had suddenly taken on a mechanical quality like a windup toy. "Why don't we talk on the way to whatever movie it is we decide we want to see?"

"No, Bob." My legs had stiffened and refused to move. The windup key had run down. "I want to talk here. To tell you the truth, I don't much feel like going out anyway." His eyes clouded briefly. "Let's go downstairs to the rumpus room, where we can be undisturbed," I added. My family had moved from our Plain Street house a few years earlier.

He followed me downstairs. The steps sounded hollow as my feet collided briefly with them. We moved toward the couch and carefully sat down. My hands traced the folds of my skirt as if they were trying to iron out imaginary wrinkles. Then I jumped up and dashed for the radio. I thought some music might help drown out the sorrow of my words. My eyes had already started to mist. "Bob," I blurted as I turned my back to the radio to face him, "I love you with all my heart, but I'm going to enter the convent."

He started to laugh at first because he thought I was joking. I always had a boisterous sense of humor. But when he saw my face, he knew I wasn't kidding. His look turned to shock.

"I have been so unfair to you," I continued. "I let this relationship develop too much and now I've hurt both you and me as a result. I am so sorry." I hung my head like a puppy that expects a slap of the paper across its nose when it's done something wrong.

"What did you say? I can't believe what I'm hearing!" he stammered.

"I said I'm going to enter the Sisters of Mercy in the fall."

He backed away from me as if I had just squirted him with Mace. I wish it had been Mace. Maybe it wouldn't have hurt so much. "Look," he said, his eyes filling up. "This thing isn't signed, sealed, and delivered yet. Let's talk about it."

We sat close together, our voices rising and falling like mountain winds that whip through empty canyons. I explained to him that entering the convent was something I had to do. I would never be happy unless I had at least tried it. Otherwise, I would always be wondering.

"We couldn't live like that," I said. "It would come back on us one way or the other. This is the only way." My anguish was complete. He pulled me close to him. Tension crackled through his body as he held me. Then, like a capricious wind that shrieks one last time before dying to a soft whisper, he suddenly let go of me.

I looked up at him. He had already turned and placed one foot on the bottom step. He pointed a finger at me and cried, "My aunt warned me about you. She never told me what it was, but I wish I had listened to her." He fled up the stairs. I heard the front door slam. I never saw him after that.

I had wanted to do good for people by entering the convent. Instead, I had hurt the very person I loved the most. After Bob left, I cried. Doing the right thing doesn't always make it the easiest thing, I concluded between sobs. Hard decisions are more often than not born from pain. But having the courage to make them in the first place is what counts.

4
NUNSENSE

"May I remind you why you are here? If you wanted to talk about boys, you should have gone to college. You're here to learn about the interior life and prayer. See that you do."

I don't recall if it was a brilliant day, a rainy day, or if the sun was falling out of the sky. But on September 8, 1961, the earth was moving under my feet. On the day that I entered the Sisters of Mercy convent, maybe it was a little bit of both: sun falling, earth turning. And all of us in my family were in a state of shock. That happens, you know, when you say good-bye.

The procession to St. Rita's had formed like a funeral caravan. Relatives' cars were lined up and followed one another at five-second intervals. It was a long and slow ride and I felt cold and clammy, as if the humidity of the day had suddenly all gathered to my skin. Everyone else tried to look comfortable, but I could also sense eyes searching the landscape, hoping to grasp something familiar and reassuring. My relatives were suspicious of nuns and what they imagined they were going to do to me. They relaxed appreciably when the convent grounds came into sight. The manicured lawns looked normal. Tall trees gathered in prayer, and shaded the driveway. Birds warbled amiably to one another, their wings beating in excitement and delight. My relatives looked at one another. Smiles forced their way through pressed lips. We drove by the Stations of the Cross and arrived at the front door. At the entrance was a stone statue of Christ. The inscription read: O BLESSED JESUS, GRANT ME THE

GRACE TO LEARN OF THEE. I wiped my brow. If this was going to be anything like my first three years of grammar school, I was in trouble.

We arrived promptly at one o'clock. I had worn one of my best dresses for the occasion, mindful that I would have to change into convent clothing at the end of the day. I rang the bell. When a senior novice answered the door, my family surrounded me like a lioness protecting her cub. The novice said that she was my earthly "guardian angel." Then she smiled at everyone and explained, "I'm supposed to take care of the postulants to make sure they don't get lost and can follow the rules." She looked squarely at me. "Arlene, my name is Sister Maria Caritas. Please follow me."

I don't know why I had expected the heavens to open at that precise moment and shower us with special blessings. Nothing happened. It was all so normal. No booming voice from above, just a simple "Follow me" from earth. We did.

"Angel" whirled on her heels, pirouetting exquisitely. I tripped over some feet, mine. She led us down the hall to one of the parlors. Half the families sat there, the other half in a similar parlor down the corridor. A huge oil portrait of Mother Catherine McAuley, foundress of the Sisters of Mercy, dominated the room, but not the conversation. Everyone was full of good-byes.

I looked around for my mom. Both of us were trying hard to hold back the tears. Good-byes are never easy in our family; this was no exception. I groped for her hand, my voice choked up. "Ma." I tried to laugh. "And you worried about me getting my clothes dirty when I was a kid. I think the only dirt we're going to have to worry about here is sin."

She couldn't say anything, but squeezed my hand in reply. Then she said, "I loved taking care of you. I feel like my whole life is walking through these doors right now." But that was all she got out.

"It's okay, Ma." I tried to soothe her pain. "This isn't the end of the world. We've got a great life together yet. It's going to be a little different now, but we'll survive." Those words could just as easily have been spoken while I was being carted off to a penitentiary. For my mother there didn't seem to be any difference. It was exile no matter how you spelled it. I gave her one last hug and followed my angel upstairs. Inside I was dying.

If Angel noticed, she didn't say anything. Even though it was a special day and an exception to the rule of silence that was otherwise vigorously observed, she kept her words to a minimum. Forty-four of us shed our worldly garments for the last time and dressed anew in black skirts that fell to the ankles, black stockings, heavy black shoes, and long-sleeved black blouses with Peter Pan collars. A half-cape that ended just below the breast clung to our shoulders much like a vulture fastened to a rock. A light black veil sheltered our hair. Edith Head would have been thrilled.

Dinner that first night was a sobering experience. None of us could believe her eyes when we walked into the refectory for our simple meal. We were supposed to sit on little stools without backs to them. I felt like Goldilocks waiting for her porridge. I had already wanted to burst into laughter several times that day but had somehow managed to contain myself. I felt my luck was running out at dinner. Eating in the convent is a solemn event. I began to grasp just how solemn when I spotted the nun in the corner. She had an impressive volume of something on her lap. Once we were all seated and had blessed our food, she started to read. It had to do with manners and nuns and what each did to the other. She read about modesty of the eyes. "They should always be downcast," she pronounced. And how to walk without swinging your arms. Swinging your arms apparently drew attention to yourself, and "Nuns, above all," she emphasized, "are not to draw attention to themselves."

I immediately broke the first rule I had just heard and looked over to one of my companions. She had the presence of mind to keep her eyes shut. If she saw me, she didn't let on. I, on the other hand, felt like a balloon that was about to be cut loose. I could feel peals of laughter welling up inside me with nowhere to go. To make matters worse, I was just the opposite of the perfect nun who had been so ardently described, and that made me want to laugh even harder, but I was also too intimidated by the seriousness of the occasion to laugh out loud.

By now my attention to manners had been distracted by the procession of food I saw brought in. It consisted of some lettuce, tomatoes, and what looked like deviled eggs. I passed it up since I wasn't big on salads. Pretty soon everybody finished eating and started washing up her dishes. What I had mistaken for salad turned out to be the entree. Not only did I have an aching heart that night; I also had an empty stomach.

You got up early in the convent. Five-fifteen A.M. and you didn't get to stay in bed rubbing your eyes and pretending that it was Sunday morning so you could sleep in. Your feet hit the floor running. While you were praying aloud to Jesus along with everybody else, you also dressed and made your bed. Next stop was chapel. You had to be in your place by five forty-five. You meditated and chanted the little office. Mass followed promptly.

Sometimes it was hard to clear your head and be fully alert that early in the morning. But I relished it. Meditation was very special to me. It was that private time of the day to gather my thoughts, retreat into the depths of my being, and nurture true spiritual growth.

After mass we had breakfast and then performed some chores before classes. One of my early duties was to gallop across the field from the novitiate to the provincial house. Six of us were assigned to general housekeeping duties there, but we had only twenty minutes in which to complete them. We usually ended up having to make two trips. We called this the "gang run" and it gave new meaning to Snoopy's Red Baron days as a fighter pilot. I'm not sure we were always right on target with the dustcloth and broom, but the running sure kept us thin if not almost always in trouble. Well-mannered nuns didn't run, at least not in the etiquette books.

I also had a problem with what the dustcloth represented. I didn't like domestic chores, thought they were a waste of time, and performed them poorly anyway. They became my cross in the convent. When you spoke about "bearing your cross," you were really talking about handling adversity. And how adversity handled you. Mostly that had to do with your interior life: learning how to put a spiritual spin on trouble, accepting the heartache, and growing as a human being. A true religious spirit required that you suffered in silence and didn't complain. I didn't complain. But I didn't find myself growing any either, as far as the "Burma Road" goes.

The Burma Road was a long, narrow, and poorly lit corridor that led past the refectory and laundry to the trunk room. It could have served as a movie set for a war story or a prison escape. The room to which it connected wasn't much better. In fact, it was worse. Everyone's belongings were stored in the trunk room. When they were put into circulation, they more or less became common property. It was my duty to keep the room clean. But it was dark and dank and cold in there. To work the trunk room wasn't a privilege, it was an agony. I shuddered every time I went in.

Convents are notoriously picky about cleanliness. Some saint a long time ago must have figured it measured the state of your soul. Since that time, it seems, convents everywhere have cleansed the spirit with a scrub brush. If this was Alice Ann's idea of finishing school, I was glad I hadn't gone to one any sooner.

OUR POSTULANCY was equivalent to the first year of college. Despite getting off to a rocky start as a youngster, I loved school as a nun. Poor penmanship, however, kept me from graduating *summa cum laude.* I got a C in calligraphy. Believe me, the way I wrote, that C stood for real Charity.

The first three months of our postulancy were a critical period. You could pretty much tell by then who would and who wouldn't last. It was, as expected, a very lonely time. All of us were suffering from homesickness. To make matters worse, even though we were forbidden to have these discussions, several of the young women with whom I had entered had more than just good religious zeal in common. We had also dated the same boys, and we discussed them at every opportunity. Consequently, we got to be very good friends. What made us good friends was the fact that we had dated them at different times.

"You really liked him?" I asked my companions. "How long did you go out before you realized the truth?" This immediately brought loud rings of laughter as each of us had some very different memories of our boyfriends.

While laughter temporarily took our minds off being homesick, it also made our lives more difficult. These were not the kinds of edifying conversations that young nuns-to-be were supposed to have, particularly when they reached the ears of the mistress of postulants. She called us into her office with a stern warning. "May I remind you why you are here? If you wanted to talk about boys, you should have gone to college. You're here to learn about the interior life and prayer. See that you do."

I wanted to learn and be prayerful, but I couldn't help but think about Bob sometimes. I wondered about him, how he was, and if he missed me. I missed him. A cousin of his had entered with me, but he never came to visit her. I hoped he would so that I could catch a glimpse of him. Within six months, however, I had settled into the business of learning the religious life and had pretty much put Bob on the back burner. I was totally on track with my earlier resolve and prepared to undergo any sacrifice to live up to it.

After one year I became a novice and received the white veil. There is a part of the ritual in which you kneel and the provincial tells you what your name in religion is. I was so nervous that I walked in and knelt on her feet. At least my arms hadn't been swinging.

Choosing and accepting a name in religion is the high point of your religious life. It was the name, above all else, that helped focus your spiritual goals. If you chose a saint's name, for example, you tried to live up to the life of that particular saint. You were told you could submit in order of choice any three Christian names you wanted, but the provincial made the final selection. It was sort of like asking for a window seat on your first airplane ride; there was no guarantee that you would get it. Not getting it was supposed to teach you humility. It was a sign of God's will and your acceptance of it. More often than not, however, it was based on how many nuns already had the name you wanted and if one more made any real difference. God worked funny. You got what was appropriate. (Nuns are now allowed to be called by their family names.)

While I was going over some appropriate names in anticipation of receiving the veil and my first habit, one of my friends began an animated discussion. I listened for a few minutes. Ginny wanted to be called Sister William Joseph, after her father.

"You know, Ginny," I said, "like you, I have prayed about this, thought about this, and searched for inspiration. I really think that I'm a Crucis [of the Cross]."

"Why do you think that?" she asked.

"Because there is a destiny to all of this. I believe that we shape our lives accordingly. We take what we have and we mold it the best way we know how. And I think that what I have to work with is in the shape of a cross."

A moment of concern flickered across Ginny's face.

I added playfully, "Not so much because I'm going to have a lot of crosses to bear in my life, but because I'm going to be a cross to a lot of other people." These words were both true and untrue. I had my share of crosses to bear as well.

Crucis must not have been a big name that year. After I knelt on her toes, the provincial awarded me with my own cross, my name. She looked at me and smiled with just the slightest hint of pain in her eyes. "And henceforth you shall be called Sister Maria Crucis." I felt I had joined my future and it was now.

Hollywood agents are not provincials, and movie stars are not nuns or priests, but there was a similar kind of magic when you slipped into what was to be for you the role of your life. Only taking vows is no make-believe part. It's the real thing.

5
RESOLUTIONS

She stuck her switchblade against my breastbone. I could feel its point. I was also getting hers.

Learning the interior life was not easy. In those days it required rigorous discipline, acts of mortification, and unbounded charity. It was easier to read Thomas à Kempis's *Imitation of Christ* than to live it. It was all part of the human condition that was denied: that unquenched seeking of the angelic among the clutter of your own simple or sometimes blinding inadequacies. As I immersed myself more deeply in the religious life, I began to suspect that the path to real spiritual glory was paved with the discarded plans of a few former perfectionists, people who saw that building on human flaws not only could be a springboard to imitating the real life of Christ, but also certainly added a realistic dimension to attaining it: converting weakness to strength, adversity to gain. For them this was the new perfection: loving their fellow human being. Maybe, I thought, these were the new saints of the new dawn in religious life. Spirituality was in change. A Vatican council had ended. Windows had been opened.

I listened to lectures about Church law and doctrine. I committed them to memory. I was forced to. I couldn't read my own handwriting. Later, while meditating, I sorted them out. It began to boil down to a simple bottom line for me: rules versus charity. Despite fresh air that had begun circulating within the Church, rules still seemed to be put ahead of people. I thought it should be the other way around.

Every moment I had that was outside required prayer and activities I spent in chapel, meditating. It was a time of great personal testing. There is perhaps no greater challenge than measuring up to yourself. Not in a conceited, self-centered way, but through the flowering of human potential. Stretching, pushing, being unafraid to extend even more, like an open field that faces the sun without shade or protection. You're willing to take the exposure.

There were mental conversations with myself, and a consideration of the deeper meaning and implication of what I was doing. It was a rewarding experience: developing a keener focus on who I was becoming, where I was going, and for what purpose.

Although I had all but put Bob out of my mind, occasionally I reflected upon what I could have had with him. These waverings of resolve, however, actually plunged me more deeply into the spiritual. Love could only be a broadening of a life committed to service of others. This restatement of purpose aided me immeasurably when I had to choose between the convent and public office.

The voyage to self-discovery is often strewn with familiar scenes. It is only when you take the time to look at them up close that you really see what they are and what they mean. The convent experience was the ultimate close-up, a magnificent high-powered telescope that beamed right into your very soul, illuminating your awakening heart.

In the convent an expected outcome of learning was the opportunity to put your lessons into practice. We were ready to serve. I eventually found myself at the training school for girls. As a junior professed nun, I had volunteered to counsel these troubled teens who had broken the law or were, for whatever reasons, incorrigible. The training school was located on the grounds of the state prison. It was decorated with barbed wire sharp enough to cut a cow in two. The idea was to keep you in. It usually worked.

One of those on the inside was only twelve years old. The second time I saw her, she was playing jacks on the floor of the main room. She was furious and cursing, the kind of words that make a sailor wince. She had just missed her eightsies. Her matted blond hair lay thick against her forehead. The rest of it was stringy and trailed to her shoulders like a package of yarn the cat had played with. Her body resembled her hair. Knees jutted out like broom handles as she squatted over her busy life. I suspected that she had been an abused child. She was wary with adults, rarely talking to them. For some reason she had made me an exception.

She saw me shadowed in the doorway. Her face broke into a grin and she ran up to me, grabbing my hand. "I've got something to show you, Sister," she said, with obvious pride in her voice. She had eyes that would just as soon break your heart as melt it. That day they were soft and vulnerable.

I waited for her. She came back with a picture of a baby, the kind you take moments after it is born. The face was all pinched up, reddish skin, no eyebrows, and eyes that squinted in disbelief that it was there at all. Somebody was holding the baby, but I just saw a pair of arms, I couldn't tell whose.

"What a nice baby!" I exclaimed, smiling at her.

She smiled back and pointed to herself. "It's my baby," she said, her face aglow.

I held my smile for as long as I could and tried to keep the lights on in my eyes. I was aghast. I could only think, What have we done to our young that forces them into these circumstances? I opened my arms and pulled her to me. I stroked her hair, but my lips could form no words. They were buried in my heart.

Then her attention waned. She skipped away from me when she saw another girl trying to make off with her jacks. There was a loud commotion as the two of them scuffled. It was over in a second. The young mother recovered her toys and began slapping the little red ball on the floor again. She was perfectly happy. I wasn't.

"Donna," I said when I got back to the convent. (Sr. Donna Carlson is a Sister of Mercy and one of my dearest friends.) "The child is a child, who has a child, and so is the system. There is no wisdom or comfort from it. It just continues to birth unworkable programs without any consequence for the future."

That little girl stuck in my mind for a long time. But there were a lot of little girls out there, all desperately needing help.

The next time I went back to the training school, I met Maria. Maria was one of those big, strong kids whose young experiences had already made them into old cynics and more than casual critics. She was boss lady, her body language spoke it, and she made sure you and everybody else never forgot it.

We had formed a circle. Everybody was given an opportunity to tell what was on her mind, if she wanted. But the only one doing the talking had been Maria.

"Hey, you know Sister Marlene, don't you?" she snarled.

"Yes, I do," I replied.

"Well, I tell you what I want you to do," she said, flinging a piece of paper on the floor. "You take that to her." She pulled her arms across her chest in a defiant stance, looking every bit like Field Marshal Rommel issuing a high command during World War II.

"Oh, you do, do you?" I said calmly. "Well, I'll tell you what, Maria. If you would like to hand me that piece of paper, I would be happy to deliver it for you. But only if you hand it to me."

Maria acted as if a bee had just stung her on a sensitive part of her body. She leaped into the air, knocking over chairs, and whipped out a shiny sharp switchblade. It was the biggest, meanest switchblade I have ever seen in my life, not that I've seen too many. It had its desired effect. The other girls rallied behind Maria. They knew how bread got sliced. I was all alone.

"Look, you," she said, "I'm telling you to take that note to Sister Marlene." She started to walk up to me like a hungry tigress stalking a quivering gazelle. She moved cautiously, one step at a time, her eyes glistening in anticipation. The room was a jungle, and like a gazelle when it tips its nose into the air and smells trouble, I stiffened all over and waited for the pounce.

Maria closed in; I hadn't moved or said anything. Squeaky voices give you away. I only hoped my eyes hadn't. She stuck her switchblade against my breastbone. I could feel its point. I was also getting hers.

She hissed at me, "Look, you. This knife says you're going to take that note to my friend." She said it in a dangerously quiet voice, all the time twisting the switchblade against my upper torso.

A million thoughts passed through my mind including whether my last confession had been good enough to get me into the next world. There was no question in my mind that that was where I was going. While I experienced varying levels of deep inner trauma, I also felt extreme anger. I never did much like people who can bully others into doing what they want, people like Maria with the big knife, or big and important people whose switchblade is their power.

"Maria," I said evenly, "I'm going to give you another chance. I think you had better pick up that note and hand it to me." My mouth closed in a straight line.

I don't know why life has constantly to be a contest of "show me your muscles and I'll show you mine." There's no need. All it does is take up valuable time and energy.

I stared real hard at Maria and she stared back and the other girls waited. Time passed. Then Maria slowly kicked a foot outward. I watched, fascinated. I hoped she wasn't getting ready to lunge at me. Then she kicked her other foot outward and slowly lowered her body to the floor. That was her way of bending down. She picked up her message and handed it to me. She wasn't used to anyone standing up to her.

Firsts are impressive no matter under what circumstances.

6
VISION AND VINEGAR

The monsignor had laid a marble floor in the gymnasium of the new school. Marble is not conducive to much of anything unless you want to pray on it. I tried to see his point of view.

The year was 1969. I was about to make final vows. I had entered the convent in 1961, studied and prayed hard. I had done what was required, lived the community life, and worked outside the convent. And now, like a pearl necklace that needs only one more strand to make it complete, I had one more decision to make. I devoted all my time to thinking about it.

It takes eight years to become a full-fledged Sister of Mercy. Final vows are no light matter. They are the biggest and strongest bolt on the door, the one you can't break to get in. Only in this case, it's the one you can't break to get out.

Preparing for final vows called for ardent prayer occasioned by a special retreat. This was a time of intense discernment and, not infrequently, the famous dark night of the soul. Nuns shuddered at ever experiencing their own personal dark night of the soul, a term used in reference to the saints whenever they were plagued by doubt and lack of resolve. But once having experienced it, it was a blessing in disguise. You had to make a decision for better or for worse. In my case, it was for the better. I loved my life as a religious. I had known it was my destiny.

The group with whom I had entered had dwindled considerably. You never knew when people were going to leave; they just weren't there the next morning. No questions were asked. None was allowed. It was seen as the hand of God; you just accepted it as fact that Her finger wasn't pointing at you. Therefore, it was with special devotion and camaraderie that my sisters and I formed a procession to the altar to recite our final vows. We had been through thick and thin together, and there was alternately great pride and humility in the knowledge that our little group had survived.

I turned to look at Sister Joseph William before we filed in. Ginny had gotten her name, all right, only in reverse. Somebody else already had the combination she had wanted. All during those formative years in the convent, the spirituality was such that nuns didn't show emotion. They practiced detachment from things and people in their headlong pursuit of sanctity. For all my easy laughter and conversation, I had wrapped myself in a mantle of religious discipline and distance. But Vatican II had torn the mantle, and human expression poured through.

I whispered, "Thank you," in Sister Joseph William's ear. We exchanged broad smiles and walked into chapel. Not only do I want to be a good nun, I thought, I really want to be a good human being.

The procession to the altar did not end there. Afterward, we took our hearts and our passion to the streets, where I believed they belonged.

I NEVER did like prejudice in any form, whether it was against people or ideas. There had been a lot of it going on when integration came to the public schools in Providence. I taught catechism to public school students at Esek Hopkins. School officials were trying to integrate Hopkins with black students from neighboring Roger Williams. Roger Williams had a bad reputation. It was tough and dangerous. Hopkins students were afraid. As a result, many students came to class with knives strapped to their legs. I encouraged my students from St. Ann's, who were sharing space at Hopkins, to eat lunch with the black students. I wanted to break down fear and, in the process, break down prejudice.

At the time this tension was growing, I had met a priest named Henry Shelton, who worked with the Catholic Inner-City Center, and who was meeting with school officials to search for ways to ease the racial strife. Henry wasn't the first priest doing inner-city work, but he certainly was the most visible and vocal. He was a real mover and shaker, and a lot of people didn't like him. He made you think. It was no surprise that when he stood up to speak at a public forum he had organized to air the issues, he didn't get the resounding applause that he deserved. In fact, he got endless boos and catcalls. Every man who had come to the microphone to speak on behalf of integration was solidly booed by the crowd.

Henry had also invited me to speak. I wasn't prepared for this bad reception, but in truth neither was the crowd prepared for me. I walked up to the microphone, awkwardly adjusted it to my level—I wasn't used to talking into microphones—and started to speak. You could have heard a pin drop. There wasn't one sound from the audience. The polite silence almost rattled me as much as the tumultuous din we had all been subjected to earlier.

"Ladies and gentlemen," I said passionately. "Look around you." My eyes danced around the room. "Who is sitting next to you? Somebody you love, somebody you hate? You're all here, aren't you, despite your feelings. And that's what we're talking about tonight, feelings. Something so powerful that they can cloud your vision and disturb your very soul. Well, I want to disturb you."

At first I thought my words had made an impact, it was so still. Then I realized it was the habit. They hadn't heard a nun speaking publicly before at an event like this. They were too polite to do anything else but listen. I learned then: so much for the power of oratory unless it comes wrapped in a black veil.

I wish I could have said the same for the Church. Nuns were nuns and priests were priests, and you always knew who was on first base.

Monsignor Anthony Dimeo was a silver-haired prelate who lived very stylishly, and who was accustomed to nuns waiting on him hand and foot. They ironed his clothes, cooked and served his breakfast, and gave Hilton Hotels a bad name for cleanliness. He expected good treatment and he got it. He was also a highly excitable individual and intimidated people through an extraordinary use of voice. He didn't just talk, he roared. When he said, "Christ died on the Cross for you," he wasn't kidding. You expected to get shipped off to jail any moment as an accessory after the fact. He was that kind of man and as a result we didn't always get along.

It had to do with the way we saw things. There are usually two ways of viewing something: yours and theirs. When you're calling the shots, you get to do it your way. When you're not, you don't. That's how it worked at the new school that was just being finished. It was alternately called Monsignor Bove Memorial (after a former pastor), or St. Ann's, depending upon your point of view. The monsignor and I tended to spar over things great and small, and not always to the credit of either of us. Take the floor, for instance.

The monsignor had laid a marble floor in the gymnasium of the new school. Marble is not conducive to much of anything unless you want to pray on it. I tried to see his point of view.

"Let me get this straight," I said with a straight face. "You've put down a marble floor because otherwise the public would be able to use it if it were a regulation floor. Is that right?"

The monsignor nodded his head pleasantly and added, "That's right. This way we keep them off it."

"Now," I continued, trying to follow his reasoning, "because it's marble, the insurance risk would be tremendous if anybody injured him- or herself playing on it. Do I have that right?"

He smiled contentedly and his eyes half closed, just like a cat's that had finished sipping a bowl of milk and had curled up on the rug.

"However, since the insurance risks would be too high, that means the school can't afford insurance. Is that right?"

By now he was literally purring. His lips curved up at the edges even more.

"What this means, of course," I struggled to continue, "is that nobody can play on it, including our own kids because we don't have insurance. So what's the point of having a gymnasium if it can't be used for the purpose for which it was intended?"

The monsignor's eyes flew open and he glared at me. Christ was dying again. When I went too far and asked if we could at least use the stage at the far end of the gym to put on a play, he stamped his foot in irritation. Not on the terrazzo marble, however. The monsignor's glare turned white hot like the inside of a volcano. His words spilled over the way hot spitting rocks do when they are hurtled from deep inside the earth. They came down hard and burning. And when he said, "No," his words scorched the air. He was afraid the stage floor might get scratched.

Bove Memorial lived up to its name. It was just that, a memorial. Eventually I was transferred. Pastors are very powerful people. Nuns are not.

I was only at St. Ann's for two years, but what truly salvaged that experience was meeting Sister Eleanor Rock. She is the director of McAuley House, the soup kitchen the Mercys run in Providence. But back then both Eleanor and I were teachers.

There are any number of different kinds of people in this world, but I bet if you had to narrow it down to two, it would be those who do and those who don't. Eleanor is a doer. Unassuming, hardworking, she is, indeed, a rock.

She was my rock during my campaign for public office. She put in long hard hours on her job and then reported cheerfully at campaign headquarters in the early morning and evenings to help me. You couldn't mistake Eleanor. She wore violet suits with big campaign pins stuck all over her lapels, and a straw hat with a bumper sticker plastered across it. She looked like a convention worker at an Iowa caucus during a presidential primary. She was also the heart and soul of my election efforts.

But more than that, she is one of the best friends I have. What she gives is more than I deserve. She helped teach me the meaning of friendship. I brought that with me to the ghetto.

7
HEARTBREAK
HOTEL

As I neared them, one of them grabbed me roughly and said, "Hey, baby! Where do you think you're going!" Frankly, I didn't have a good answer for that. I was numb with fear.

I don't subscribe to the theory that you have to be really down before you know which way is up. On the other hand, unless you can walk in someone else's shoes, you don't always know how they fit. And so it was with the ghetto. I knew I wanted to pursue a ministry serving the poor. I had worked Saturdays at the Catholic Inner-City Center in South Providence. I had some inkling of the problems and the people. After final vows I was sent there to work full time.

There was a group of us who wanted to do more, however. We wanted to be a part of the community in which we were working. We asked to live in the ghetto, to get firsthand knowledge of what life among the poor and disadvantaged was really like in order to serve them better. It was appropriate, we thought, because we were supposed to be poor, too. We even had a vow of poverty to prove it. It was also a way of gaining trust from people who didn't know the meaning of it, had never extended it, and probably had never witnessed it.

The provincial at the time was a farsighted woman, Mother Kiernan Flynn. She approved of our request. She had a fire burning in her belly, too. It squared with her own values of reaching out to people no matter what the cost. We were the first nuns in Rhode Island to live outside our convent setting. All eyes were watching us as we trotted off with our meager belongings to live in a housing project on Hartford Avenue in Providence.

There were five of us. Two had doctorates and were professors at Salve Regina College in Newport. Another also taught at Salve and had a master's in public health nursing. The fourth was Sister Donna Carlson, who was a teacher in a ghetto school. We lived on what it would cost a welfare family of five to survive. Any other money we earned went back to the order.

Our apartment cost forty dollars a month. It was on the top floor of one of the double-deckers. It was cold and dank. Paint chippings the size of folded tissue paper dotted the floor. The walls were scarred and bare. The ceiling had big rust spots on it where water must have leaked continuously without repair. It was like a cement tomb.

Living in the project wasn't quite what I had expected it to be. It was worse. All the buildings looked as if the Allies had bombed them not once but twice during World War II, America's version of Dresden, Germany. We stared at one another for what seemed a full five minutes. Sister Janice Cowsill gulped the loudest. The noise of her choking broke the ice and we all burst out laughing.

"What do you think your mother would say right now if she could see this mess?" Janice asked.

"Arlene, I told you to clean up your room!" I blurted.

Home it was not, but home it was to be for two years. In all, other nuns and I lived fifteen years in the ghettos, trying to bring a better quality of life to the people.

The people who lived in the Hartford project started to get used to us after a while. At first they didn't quite know what to make of our modified habits: navy-blue dresses to the knees, and black veils. They probably thought we had been too poor to afford the real thing. Clothes weren't so much a barrier, however, but attitudes were. Suspicions ran deep. People weren't too interested in their fellowman; they had been ripped off enough. Building up community values and community pride, which was my job, was like trying to raise the *Titanic* with a piece of string. It didn't seem that it would work, but we did what we could. I tried to organize the people, find out what their needs were, and talk about their problems.

One night, not too long after we had moved in, the five of us sat talking. It was one of those let-down-your-hair sessions. The place had already begun to get to us: Our collective spirit had fallen like the temperature on a cold New England day.

Even Donna, who has the heart and soul of one of God's special beings, felt a slight, uncharacteristic chill.

Janice gazed at her steadily for a moment. "I think your sense of worth gets beaten out of you. But it's understandable. Look what we're feeling. We're developing all the classic symptoms of the downtrodden. It's just plain depressing. This place *is* upsetting."

"You know," Donna said, "I look around me and I can't believe this kind of misery, that people actually live this way, seem to get used to it, and, worse yet, have no desire to do anything about it." Then a warm smile spread across her face. "You know, sisters, no matter what we're feeling, we're pretty lucky; we've got each other. That's more than a lot of people can say, and knowing that gives me enormous comfort because I couldn't do it by myself. I need you, you need me, we need each other."

Maybe that's what is so marvelous about the Mercy spirit. You know what the odds are, and knowing that, you still plunge ahead.

Every so often you can pinpoint experiences that shape your character and your destiny. Living in the projects was one of them. There were times, like that night, when I felt unsure, but all I had to do was look around me, as Donna had said, to see who was there. It didn't always erase doubt, but it did make the living more bearable.

However, I never did get used to the hollering and screaming that went along with the brawling, drinking, and drugs. Domestic fights, not bliss, were as frequent as the popping sounds beer cans make when they are opened in the dark of night. Those were the quiet arguments. Other times, they sounded like shotguns going off and probably were.

IN EVERY tragedy there is a real face to put to the statistic. I had made friends with an old woman from the ghetto. She was uneducated and vulnerable, but fiercely independent. She had a marvelous sense of herself and found, what was for her, real joy in her daily outings. Every day she took the bus downtown. These forays away from the project helped define her spirit and gave her purpose. I had become very fond of her. One day, while waiting for the bus, she got mugged by a teen-ager. She was knocked down and her hip was broken and she wound up having to move to a nursing home. She had come to trust me and so I had the unenviable task of cleaning out her apartment. It wasn't difficult. There wasn't much to put away for her. Her life amounted to a few pictures, a few pieces of furniture, and a few souvenirs from trips to places in better times. But the good times had ended for her. The system of justice hadn't been just. While she was consigned to a nursing home the rest of her life in what truly amounted to a life sentence, her assailant had gotten off with a slap on the wrist.

I never forgot that. When I became attorney general, I remembered my elderly friend. My first piece of legislation had her name on it. I got a law passed allowing people's entire record, including the tab they had run as juvenile offenders, to be weighed against them when they committed crimes as adults. I felt both of us had been sprung from the nursing home.

* * *

YOU COULDN'T always make a direct impact on people's lives in the project, but you could sure try to influence management to improve conditions. Although there were garbage chutes on the sides of each building, they were neither big enough nor long enough to do the job. Garbage piled up and attracted animals. The rats were so big in that place you could throw saddles on them. We agitated to get things cleaned up, and succeeded. We also got all the refrigerators fixed. None of them had worked well and had always broken down. Food was wasted and so was money. It seems the poor always pay more for the basics than do the rich.

Sometimes, however, it is through the tangible that real change from within can come. I don't think any of us could judge back then whether a firm conversion of the spirit had taken place in the lives we touched, but seeing physical improvements in your life usually helped open the door to hope.

While we were hoping to teach others, others taught us. One night I came home late. There's such a thing as coming home late and coming home late in the projects. Neither is a good idea. It was under cover of night that the worst drinking and brawling and drug use occurred. But if the people were fairly sober and nonbelligerent, I could usually slip by them without too much trouble. My nun's status helped smooth the way. But it was a good distance from where we parked the cars to our door, and trouble stood in between.

Four big men blocked my way. They were high on something, and instead of feeling good, they were feeling mean. By the time I realized it, they had already spotted me. I had a choice of turning around and going back the way I had come, going around them, or going through them, since they were standing on what appeared to be a sidewalk. If I turned tail, they would go for me. If I went around them, they would become even bolder. But if I proceeded walking as I was, straight for them, that might give me the advantage of surprise. I didn't think they would expect that. My heart had dropped from my chest to my knees and was knocking against them. This was certainly one of those times I wished I had listened to my mother. But if you find yourself knee-deep in water, pick up a bucket and start bailing.

I sucked in my breath and plunged ahead. As I neared them, one of them grabbed me roughly and said, "Hey, baby! Where do you think you're going!" Frankly, I didn't have a good answer for that. I was numb with fear. My usual toothy smile seemed locked in a frozen grin.

Somehow I managed to summon a little presence of mind. Breaking his grasp with a solid twist of my arm, I said, "Gentlemen, there's no doubt that you are stronger than me, and that there are more of you. Now that I've acknowledged your power, we really don't have anything to argue about, or, for that matter, to talk about. Now kindly get out of my way because I've got places to go and people to see."

Their mouths dropped in astonishment. They had been looking for a fight and didn't get one. The four looked at one another blankly and then parted like the waters of the Red Sea. At that moment, however, I did not feel like Moses, or even remotely like Charlton Heston. I couldn't wait to get upstairs. Unbeknown to them, they had succeeded in putting the fear of God into me.

I'm not sure that it was the smartest thing I did, maybe it was the luckiest thing, but in any event it seemed to be the right thing.

MY EXPERIENCES in the Hartford housing project taught me that really to effect change, I needed to acquire some different skills. I had seen on a daily basis the denial of consumer rights to people who had bought shoddy furniture and appliances because that was all they could afford. Chairs broke and stores refused to replace them or give people their money back. Some of the nuns and I also stood for hours with people trying to get something done about their phone and utility bills. It was always the same: The law says this, you can't do that. But more than anything, I had seen that there was a different system of justice for the poor. The rights of the powerful didn't trickle downward. I wanted to open up the waterworks. I decided I wanted to be a lawyer. The profession seemed to give you the tools to help people in the most fundamental and, ultimately, powerful way.

I approached my superior, Mother Kiernan Flynn. We met in her office at the provincialate in Cumberland. It was quiet and comfortable and totally unlike the ghetto. For the moment, like a cool wave that washes over you in summer, it felt good to be there.

"Mother, I know that this is an unusual request. Nobody from our province has ever gone to law school. We've always dealt in service to people through hospitals, teaching, and social service work. But I think a legal background is an excellent avenue to pursue, too. It speaks to what we do best, filling the unmet need. The law is so powerful that it can literally change the way we act and think. We can also replace bad laws with good laws. And where the law is unclear, we can give it focus for good purposes that serve people."

My superior listened attentively. "As you know, dear Sister, this must go before the administrative team. I'll be back to you." She gave me a reassuring smile.

I didn't have to wait too long. I was told that if I passed the entrance exam, I could attend.

I went to Brown University and took the Law School Aptitude Test. I had no time to prepare for it. Instead of praying that I would know the answers to the questions, I prayed God would fudge and perform a small miracle, such as appearing in a dream to the computer grading my exam. That computer would be instantly instructed to award me not only a passing mark, but a decent passing mark.

God must have been paying a lot of attention that day. I applied to and was accepted at Boston College. The ladies' room had become larger.

8
LAWYERS AND LESSONS

"Lady," he said, "I'm the owner's son and what this salesman has told you is the absolute truth. It's a five-hundred-dollar rebate, not a thousand dollars. You're just not reading the ad right."

I loved law school and I think it loved me. While it had its difficult moments, it was pretty much the opposite of everything I thought it would be. It was exciting when I thought it would be boring, stimulating instead of dreary, and sustaining when it could have been empty. I was like the proverbial kid in the candy store. I didn't know which piece of confection to pick up first. It all looked so good.

There were 250 people in my class, 15 of whom were women, including me. Word had gotten around pretty fast that I was a nun. Looks of interest were thrown my way as some people steal glances at chocolate under glass in a sweetshop. Too much interest can ruin the diet.

I had a rigorous schedule but I thrived on it. During the week I lived in Newton, Massachusetts, with the Religious of the Sacred Heart nuns, and on the weekend in Rhode Island with my own community of nuns. I had to get up at five-thirty to attend classes all day long. Then I came back to the convent for mass, the community meal and recreation, and study until eleven o'clock. I took as many courses as possible over and beyond the courses in which I had exams. I wanted to learn everything there was to take maximum advantage of my three years in law school. If learning were water, I was a sponge.

One of my favorite courses was commercial law. It involved consumer issues. I was selected to be one of the students to work with William Willier, who ran the National Consumer Law Center at Boston College, where research was done for Ralph Nader. It was the beginning, the cutting edge for developing an expertise in consumer law.

Law wasn't all that I was learning. School may be a great avenue for debate and the exchange of ideas, but it can also be a gigantic warehouse of human problems. Boston College was no exception. Increasingly, many of my classmates began unloading more than case histories on me. Marriages were coming apart under pressure; competition, both real and artificial, was taking a grim toll; and humiliation seemed an expected casualty on this mental battlefield for one-upmanship.

I listened for hours as classmates told me how difficult it was to balance the needs of their partner with the pressures of law school. It was such an intense time that they felt every spare moment had to go for extra studying. That left the other half of the relationship feeling neglected. Consequently, there was a lot of pain and a lot of self-absorption. For many it came down to a choice: law school or the relationship.

These students had sought me to tell me their most private thoughts. I think it was because I was a nun; I wasn't a threat. Nuns were supposed to pray for you, not take advantage of you. In the fiercely competitive environment of law school, you never wanted to give an opponent the edge. Self-revelation could be your undoing as well as your unburdening. I used to help these students with their notes and loan them my books if they needed them.

One time I saw a friend of mine, Paul, nearly in tears. He wasn't sad; he was angry.

"You won't believe this! I go to the library to bone up on a case and somebody has ripped out the pages. What animal would do that?" he screamed.

Instead of bringing out the best in people, law school seemed to bring out the worst in some. Not only did students try to do each other in, but several professors had a policy of deliberately flunking 50 percent of their class, no matter what. Others humiliated their students under the pretense that judges in real courtrooms did it all the time. "You've got to learn to take the heat," they reasoned. "We're doing you a favor by weeding you out now. If you can't take it here, you won't survive there."

I began to suspect what many of the public think now, that there's a lot of space between lawyers and ethics. Maybe law school is what helped put the distance there.

During the summers I worked at Rhode Island Legal Services, helping low-income clients and defraying my law school costs at the same time. One day a woman came to see me whose son had psychiatric problems.

"Sister," she said, "I've got this son who needs help bad. And I've got him in Butler Hospital." This was a privately run psychiatric facility in Providence. "They thought I had some medical insurance to cover the expenses. I thought I had it, but it turns out I don't, and now they want to kick him out."

I had been reading about cases as a student and had a real opportunity to put flesh and blood to what I had learned. The distraught mother and I arrived at Butler Hospital. We were ushered into the conference room. A lot of important-looking people stared at us. "Madam," they said, "we are sorry to inform you that while your son is quite seriously psychiatrically ill, he cannot remain here. He'll have to go." Where to seemed to be the state psychiatric facility.

I piped up, "You take him out of here and you're going to have quite a legal battle on your hands. By your own admission, he's quite ill." My voice was a little higher than normal and sounded like it was missing a syllable every other word.

"How do you figure that, ah, ah—"

"Sister Violet," I finished for them. "Why don't you tell me about the treatment program you have in mind for him at the state facility."

"Well, actually," one of the doctors explained, "we're not familiar with any programs that might be available for him there."

"Let me get this straight," I said. I had found my voice. I was also beginning to feel like Florence Nightingale in the midst of battle. "You want the boy out of here, but you can't tell me what possible good that's going to accomplish other than it's not going to cost you. Well, gentlemen, I think that's a highly debatable matter, and one the courts will certainly find mighty interesting, if not despicable. Don't you agree?"

To the credit of the doctors and hospital committee, there was a decided change of mind. The boy stayed and was treated. One of the doctors at the meeting that day was the son of a Rhode Island Supreme Court justice.

A day or so later I got a call from Judge Thomas Paolino's secretary. I was invited to interview with the judge for a law clerk position he was offering following my graduation from law school. We talked, he offered, I accepted. It was a valuable experience and gave me great insight into the workings of the court and the individual judges. I learned the thought processes of the court, why some arguments failed and others succeeded. This knowledge was particularly important to me as a lawyer fighting for my own cases. Like a rookie baseball player, I was able to watch the game up close and learn from the mistakes of others.

In 1974, I became the first Rhode Island nun to graduate from law school. A Mercy nun in the Midwest also graduated the same year. What we had ushered in became commonplace in the ensuing years.

CLERKING FOR Judge Paolino was a full-time job. As a law clerk you were supposed to read and research cases so that you could offer the justices legal opinions on those cases under consideration. I was responsible for twenty-five cases that would be argued during the first week of every month the court was sitting. That meant I had to know them inside out, the pros and cons, and whether there was sound legal principle that justified their being before the court in the first place. Oral arguments were like a prize fight, a real give-and-take of the mental muscles, a sharp jab to a legal mistake here and a slow punch to avoid a fundamental weakness there. The judges scored the match.

A case of particular interest to me concerned the dividing of a heart. It was a nasty divorce. The husband and wife had ended up not liking each other a long time ago. Their case went to court and then to another court. The woman said her husband had been cruel, but her lawyer never proved that there was any physical impact of that cruelty, a necessary element for that grounds for divorce in Rhode Island. The lower court had denied the divorce on the grounds that no physical element had been shown.

I read the case and researched all the legal components. It occurred to me that there was indeed a physical element. Mental cruelty can produce all kinds of physical side effects, for example, stress on the body, which is a physical impact. I recommended that the divorce be granted. Judge Paolino didn't buy my argument, but the justices who rendered the minority opinion used it. Just like in the ring, it was a split decision, 3 to 2.

Now mind you, this was 1974 Rhode Island, a state that is sometimes more Catholic than the Vatican. Here I was, a nun, drafting an opinion granting a divorce, the principle of which has never been recognized by the Church. On the one hand I had before me the dogma and practices of the Church, on the other, legal principles that were equally compelling. Actually more so, because the arena of decision was a court of law, not St. Peter's Basilica. Writing that opinion was a very crucial experience for me and helped lay the foundation for future decisions I was called upon to make. I recognized that while opinions may not be popular or even adopted, it is important to make them on the basis of good sound legal judgments.

I clerked from July 1974 to May 1975, when Attorney General Julius Michaelson hired me as a special assistant attorney general to run his consumer division. I was the first nun in the country to be so appointed. I had applied for the job in December after his election. He had run a campaign built on consumer issues. I brought over to the interview all my credentials and recommendations from law school, including my work with the National Consumer Law Center.

"I'm really serious about putting together a first-rate consumer division," he had said in so many words. "I like what you've got here. Do you think you can do the job?"

I think I had mumbled something like "Is the Pope Catholic and do you mind if I dress the way I do with this big cross around my neck?" I figured that when you're out there fighting vampires who are preying on innocent consumers, you've got to dress the part. If silver crosses work in Transylvania, they should work in Rhode Island.

I was ecstatic. I shared the good news with my mom. "You'll never guess what," I said. "I'm finally going to get a chance to do what I've always wanted to do since those early days of living in the projects. I'm going to head up the consumer protection unit at the AG's office!" My mom threw her arms around me and we both held each other close.

The unit was in disarray when I arrived. Most of the people

working there had no formal training in consumer matters. I opted for a quick crash course in the basics. I was reminded of my young-nun days coaching a ragged Little League team to dubious victory. It had been unglorious and, to some who didn't think we should have been playing at all, unpopular, but we had done it anyway. I had another opportunity to exercise some real constructive leadership in an area that seriously needed it.

A week later our first big case came up. A local chain drugstore had offered an "up to 50 percent off" sale. But you had no way of knowing what percent the drugstore was really taking off. Was it 1 percent, which was also up to 50 percent, or was it 49 percent, or 25? The company didn't say. We thought it should. I spoke to its president.

"Sir," I said, "your ad is not exactly clear, and unless you can stipulate what percent, in fact, your sale represents, I'm afraid you'll have to pull the ad."

There was silence and then a polite cough followed by "Do you know who I am?"

"Yes, I do."

"Well, you may think you know who I am, but I'm also a big contributor to your boss. So I think you had better rethink what you just told me."

"Actually," I said very carefully, "the choice is up to you. You can either appear in Superior Court tomorrow morning at nine-thirty with your lawyers, or you can pull your ad. You decide. I've already made my decision. I'm going to file a Deceptive Trade Practices action against you to stop you from doing business in this manner."

The man at the other end of the phone made a call to my boss to try to stop me. It didn't work. The ad was pulled, and now the consumer unit was the one in business. By the time I had left the unit after sixteen months, we had returned to the consumer $1.2 million in cash, goods, and services.

Another time, a Mazda dealership ran an ad that offered

$1,000 off the purchase price of any of its cars. Five hundred off the sticker price and five hundred back from the factory. At that time I was living in Warwick, and the nuns with whom I shared a house needed a car. I had seen the ad and suggested that we take a drive down to do some shopping.

"Well, what can I do for you little ladies?" one of the salesmen said.

"We've come to see about the thousand-dollar offer that's being advertised," I responded.

A big grin split his face. "Oh, no, that's not a thousand dollars. It's five hundred dollars. Everybody's been reading that ad wrong." He rubbed his hands together, waiting.

"No, it's actually a thousand dollars," I repeated.

"Honey," he said and draped his arm around my shoulders confidentially, "a lot of women have trouble reading that ad, like I just told you. Isn't that right?" he said, turning around and gesturing to another man to come over.

The other man came over. Same big grin. "Lady," he said, "I'm the owner's son and what this salesman has told you is the absolute truth. It's a five-hundred-dollar rebate, not a thousand dollars. You're just not reading the ad right."

The other nuns stared at their shoes.

"Well, I tell you what," I said, scratching my chin thoughtfully, "if the owner is here, I would like to speak to him."

It just so happened he was. He joined our widening group.

"What's the story on this rebate business? Is it true what these men are telling me?" I queried.

The owner repeated word for word what the first two had told me.

"You know, I originally came here because my friends and I were interested in buying a car. I'm not interested in buying a car now. I'm interested in taking you to court. I head up the consumer unit at the Department of Attorney General." I showed them my credentials.

There were audible gasps all around. The smiles came off their faces as easily as an eraser wipes chalk marks from a blackboard.

I looked at them. "You come down at nine-thirty tomorrow morning and we'll see who understands what. You'll have plenty of opportunity to explain it to the judge." I paused a moment to let that sink in. "I'll tell you what else I'll do, just to make this less traumatic for you. You can either go to court, or you can do a smarter thing and appear in my office tomorrow morning with all your documentation on how many consumers you've been ripping off. Your lawyers in court, or you in my office. The choice is yours."

They appeared in my office bright and early the next day with all the invoices I had requested and the names of everybody who had been sold a Mazda in the two weeks that the ad had been running. That came to forty-two cars, or $21,000. I felt like Sara Lee when her first cake was baked. Only my joy came from dividing it up.

On another occasion a man and his wife ran an insurance scheme that deprived elderly participants of any insurance coverage. They got the seniors to cash in their old insurance policies, which they'd had for years and years, in order to buy whole life insurance the man sold to them at a substantial commission. Then he told them that if they bought a certain mutual fund, the dividends from the fund would pay off their insurance premiums. Naturally, he sold them the mutual fund for another good commission. In practice, however, the dividends didn't cover the premiums and the insurance policies lapsed, leaving the seniors uninsured. Because of their age, they were also uninsurable if they wanted to try to pick up another policy.

These vulnerable seniors truly had been victims of crime just as if someone had broken into their homes and robbed them blind. I was angry. We sued everybody who had been a part of the scheme. We went after the man and his wife in particular.

During court one day, I questioned the wife while she was on the stand. She had stated earlier that she had attended all the sessions with her husband and the clients and that she had a photographic memory. Her point was that her husband had never stated to their clients that the dividends would cover their premium payments.

I began, "You claim that you have a photographic memory, is that right?"

She nodded her head vigorously and snapped, "Yes, I do."

"You remember precisely the conversations that occurred at the Austin house, and all the ensuing business? Every detail?"

"Indeed, I do," she stated emphatically, eyes breezing around the courtroom in triumph before they came back to rest on me. She exhaled noisily, as if by divine right.

I put her through nine or ten more cases. Each time she confirmed her observations. "Yes, I remember that. It's exactly as I told you."

All throughout this exchange, I had been holding a piece of paper. I creased it between my fingers, saying, "You've been sitting in this courtroom for three days now. And since you have a photographic memory, how many lights are in the chandelier above your head?"

Then I dropped the paper and stooped to pick it up. Her head shot upward, eyes rotated to the ceiling to count the lights. "Seven," she said.

That was all the members of the jury needed to see. They returned a guilty verdict.

AFTER A long day busy with consumer problems, I retreated to Warwick. The other nuns and I tried to spend time together, but our schedules were so hectic it wasn't always possible. Even though we shared a house, it seemed as if we barely saw one another. Once in a while, however, we did connect and on those occasions we shared dreams and common goals. It was the only time I really had to relax.

One time I looked around at my friends with a sense of awe. There we were, the same hardworking crew from our young-nun days. But had time changed us? I spoke to the nun sitting nearest me, the sister of my good friend, Donna Carlson. "How do you feel about yourself and your life? Did it all come out the way you thought, Dianne?" I wrinkled my nose at her. "Were you successful in making changes where you wanted?"

Dianne Carlson was the most philosophical of all of us. As a teacher she knew how to bring to any level of understanding the most complicated of all issues, ourselves. She studied her hands for a moment before replying. They were brown from the summer sun and rough and dry from erasing too many chalkboards. "What I have grown into," she said simply, "is my own skin." She raised her head, eyes twinkling.

I studied my hands a moment before showing them to her. "I'm getting there."

9
SKIN TIGHT

"Being a nun is more important to me than anything in this world. Beyond this world. It is life to me itself."

While I had been growing into my skin, I had made somebody else jump out of his. True to my religious name of Crucis, I had lived up to my prophecy that I would become another's cross. His name was Bishop Daniel Cronin. The issue was a day-care facility in Fall River, Massachusetts, the bishop's home turf. The bishop was the landlord of this particular day-care center, St. John's Child Care and Development Center, but I served on its board. As a lawyer I had been able to serve on a number of out-of-state boards as long as they didn't interfere with my principal responsibilities at the attorney general's office. As it happened, I had rotated into the position of board president at a time when a dispute with the day-care center lease came up, although what it came down to was money.

Even though we had a three-year lease with a renewable option, we had heard that the bishop wasn't going to renew it. He could get more for the property by renting it to somebody else. We weren't going to be that somebody else. Before we could get our dander up, we were shot down. The bishop put a padlock on the door. We were effectively locked out.

It couldn't have come at a worse time. Fall River had one of the highest unemployment rates in the country. Former welfare mothers, many of them single, whose children were under the center's care worked from dawn to dusk to make ends meet.

Those were the lucky ones, the ones who had jobs. They looked to us to take care of the children. They had no other place to turn.

I knew that under Rhode Island law it was illegal to lock out somebody without due process. I checked Massachusetts law. It was the same. The bishop didn't have grounds, but we did. The corporate boardroom had taken up a new address and I had to sue the chairman of the board.

I spoke to Judge Milton Silva, a Portuguese and a devout Catholic. He wrung his hands, wailing, "I can't believe this. You're a Catholic, I'm a Catholic, and he's a Catholic. You're a nun, I'm a judge, and he's a bishop. A nun suing a bishop in such a Catholic community as Fall River!"

I felt sorry for the judge. I could just hear him thinking to himself, If there's a way to get to heaven, this isn't it.

But the judge did grant the complaint, and ordered the bishop to reopen the center. It had been an unauthorized lockout. The bishop refused to turn over the key. We considered a picket line.

I talked it over with Sister Kate Harrington, one of our nuns who ran the center. "Look, Kate," I said, half smiling, "you and I have been down many roads together, long and narrow, straight and bumpy, but this is one of the toughest yet." I had been thinking of the times other nuns and I had picketed in front of the governor's mansion, a mayor's office, and banks that were redlining housing districts. It had always been the same. Members of the Church hierarchy tried to get us reassigned because we were shaking the pillars of society. Their society.

Kate was bent over a small child, pushing arms into, I thought, the tiniest coat I had ever seen. I wasn't much with the little ones, but they loved her. She straightened up.

"Arlene, what do we stand for if not for the people? It isn't religious authority we're here to protect, it's religious freedom. But religious freedom is based on economics." Kate, who is Irish, said, "Look at Ireland. They tell you it's religious, but in fact it's an economic war over there. You have a job; I don't. You have money; I don't. Give me what you have. If you don't, I'll take it. Now the bishop is calling upon Church principle to make us toe the line. In this case, obedience. But he's denying the foundation on which people are governed, and that's the pocketbook."

"Actually, the bishop understands economics very well," I said ruefully.

Our eyes locked briefly. There had been no other choice. The picket lines had to go up. Call it an act of courage, or an act of stupidity. After all, we were allegedly defying Mother Church, our refuge and our salvation. It was not lost on us, however, that men of power in the Church claimed their authority under the auspices of a woman.

I stood rigidly outside the day-care center, eyes focused on the gleaming padlock. It sealed off a large room that had housed so many hopes for so many desperate women. I wanted to take a blowtorch to the lock. Instead, my anger flared. "We are really on the high wire this time," I fumed. "Only I'm not going to walk it and hope I don't fall. I'm going to dance my way across."

The picket lines went up. We joined hands with the mothers, and the women started to dance, as in some ancient rite heralding a common identity. There was purpose and, at the same time, a strange energy that emanated from our small group. It spread to others and the group grew. Soon the news media arrived, television cameras rolling, to record for brief posterity women defying the authority of the Church. But the media had missed the point. It wasn't defiance of authority that was at stake here, it was preservation of life, the ability of women to earn money to feed and clothe their children.

Two days after I had signed the complaint requesting a restraining order, the bishop threatened Kate and me with excommunication. The Rhode Island nuns stood behind us, the Massachusetts nuns stood apart. We were sisters of the cloth, but apparently not completely in spirit.

Bolts of sadness shot through me with the swiftness of light-
ning from a summer storm. I could understand what was passing through the other nuns' minds. They, too, had valuable
ministries to which they were dedicated. But life, very often, is
compromise. The secret is knowing when it works and when it
doesn't. Kate and I didn't believe that this was one of those
instances where compromise worked.

The provincial called me for a meeting. "Look, Sister," she
said. "We've got a very real problem here. You are openly
defying the bishop, and it's bad for the Church to see a nun
fighting with the bishop. It sends out the wrong message, particularly since the media have portrayed him as a ruthless landlord."

"He is a ruthless landlord," I said.

"He is our bishop and God's representative on earth," she
countered.

"He's nothing more than an ecclesiastical blackmailer."

I had gone too far. A warning light came on in her eyes, but
she continued tapping her forefinger on the writing blotter.
"You've got a legitimate issue," she said evenly, "but unfortunately this issue is going to have an enormous impact on the work
of the other nuns. Not only will they be forced to abandon their
work because the bishop won't allow them to continue, but they
may be asked to leave the diocese as well. All will be threatened
by the consequences of your actions."

She hesitated for a minute and said carefully, "I'm asking you
to give this up. If you don't willingly, then I'm going to order
you, under holy obedience, to conform. I'll give you a few days
to think about it."

I unconsciously looked at my hands. "Mother Mary Mercy,
your point is well taken. But I think we've got a shark on our
hands. We keep pacifying the bishop and he's never satisfied."

Her eyes didn't leave mine.

I continued, "Now it's the day-care center, and others unconnected to it are being threatened. What will it be tomorrow? The shark keeps getting hungrier."

"The bishop has directed me to tell you that he expects a decision from you and Kate no later than Friday. I'm sorry, Sister," she said softly, "there isn't any more time. Your day of judgment is here. Please, for all of us, back off this just once so that others can continue what is important to them, and you can avoid excommunication."

I had a big knot in my throat. I tried swallowing hard a few times, but the lump didn't get any smaller. I opened my mouth, forcing the words to come out. "Being a nun is more important to me than anything in this world. Beyond this world. It is life to me itself." I noticed that my hands were trembling. That was when I realized that my body had been shaking all over.

My eyes rested on a crucifix that hung on the wall just over the provincial's shoulder. I said slowly, "My identity is carved inside of me in the shape of a cross. My spirit is wed to my heart. And my heart beats for one purpose only, to serve the unmet need, to restore to life those who have been broken by it."

My gaze dropped to Mother Mary Mercy's face. "I'd rather be a Sister of Mercy in reality than a Sister of Mercy in name only. I've lived in the inner city, I know what these people are about. I've stood with them before, and I guess I'm going to stand with them again. When they look around to see who's with them, I want them to see me."

I climbed into my car for the long ride home. I heard the pounding surf in my ears, then the ocean washed over my face. My tears tasted very salty.

There was no showdown that Friday. The letters-to-the-editor page of the local newspaper had been full of messages about me, people thanking me for the good work of my consumer unit on their behalf. The timing couldn't have been better. Being a bishop also means having to stick your finger into the political winds to see which way they are blowing. There was a gale-force wind out there and it wasn't blowing against me. The bishop quietly dropped any talk of excommunication.

We eventually built a new center, the John Boyd Center, which we named after the priest who had gotten the original lease for us in the first place. Kate, my very talented, bright friend, who sits on many influential boards and commissions in Massachusetts, also knew a lot of important people back then. Tip O'Neill, John McCormack, and Carl Albert came out to help in the fund-raising effort. I don't know if they visited the bishop.

Kate and I did, however. We were ushered into his private office. It was magnificent in its appointments, but not overly comfortable, as if someone were afraid you would actually want to stay. But to both the initiated and uninitiated alike, the room as a whole was impressive. Large pictures of our Lord and various Church officials dotted the walls. This was clearly a man's room.

The bishop began first, and didn't seem to want to stop. His pink biretta perched at an angle on his head. It seemed brighter than usual, matching the color in his face. His knuckles were peaks of white in his folded hands.

"You are both a disgrace to the Church," he thundered. "You have humiliated her, confused the people and led them astray, and destroyed any capacity for the proper recognition of authority. In short, you two are a scandal."

We had known this wasn't going to be an easy meeting. I was getting more uncomfortable by the minute. Nobody likes to be chewed out by anybody, particularly when it's a somebody like the bishop. Kate and I glanced at each other. The same thought had crossed our minds. The anybodys never got to be somebodys, and the somebodys weren't about to make room for the anybodys.

"Meaning no disrespect, your Excellency," I said in a quiet voice, "bishops and nuns do have something in common. Neither is *the* authority. Each is only a voice of authority. That authority comes from God. Our purpose here is to serve the people, not each other." I knew that as far as the bishop was concerned, we had been treading on some thin theological ground having to do with holy obedience. From his perspective, I could only imagine that a pencil line separated Kate and me from signing our names in hell's register.

I continued anyway. "If we are truly here to serve people, then we've got to stand with them, not on top of them."

Bishop Cronin's eyes narrowed. He had become visibly angry. "You are incorrigible and the two of you are very poor nuns." He practically spat out the words. "It's very obvious that you possess not the slightest understanding of what the Church is or your role in it."

But it was a new era in the Church, post-Vatican II, when change was the order of the day, and obedience an issue for revision.

We stood up to leave. "You can dismiss us, your Excellency," I said, "but you can't dismiss reality. You may be shepherd of your flock, but you're not master of our souls."

It wasn't a victory; it wasn't even a meeting of minds. It was like witnessing what happens when a gun is fired on a target range. There is a loud noise and sometimes a puff of smoke, but you can't see the bullet. You can only hope that it will eventually hit the bull's-eye.

10
DIASPORA DAYS

Dianne shook her head. "I believe God keeps pushing the pencil our way for us to write our own destiny, but we keep pushing it back."

My days heading the consumer unit at the attorney general's office had come to a close. I had plenty of firepower left, but my order had certain needs that required attending. Fighting for the rights of others was one objective, but in those days I believed that when it came to your own personal destiny, humility required that your life be a blank page upon which the will of God was written. In that sense, events shaped you; you didn't shape them. When all the Mercys met in Providence for their election of regional officers and the formation of policy on major issues, my name had been placed in nomination for a slot on the administrative team. It was shortly after my brush with the bishop. I was convinced that life often resembled a seesaw. One minute you were up, the next you weren't.

"My sisters," I said, "I want you to know that I am tremendously honored that you would think so highly of me. Bishop Cronin pleaded with me to allow him to write a letter of reference on my behalf, but I ended up declining on the basis that when I went over to his residence to pick it up, the door would be padlocked."

The nuns screamed in delight.

"But I want you to know that through honor comes conflict. I'm a street fighter, not a bureaucrat. I'm more comfortable on picket lines than behind picket fences. I truly believe that we are the Church in diaspora, on the move. We don't wallpaper our tents, we just pick them up and cart them off to someplace new."

I looked around at my sisters. They were hushed and expectant. I really liked working in the trenches. Desk jobs weren't for me. I added, "We've got a lot of talented people in our province. I would hope that you would reconsider my nomination in favor of them."

Nuns are cantankerous people. They never do what you expect. I was elected vice provincial.

I had to resign from the attorney general's office. My new challenge was to get the Sisters of Mercy on firm financial footing, because in addition to being vice provincial I was also the treasurer. I was responsible for all the business dealings and investments of the province, including management of the Mercys' property holdings.

The Mercys had been undergoing some tough times. Our investments and other income hadn't produced enough to cover our debts. We also had a pension plan in theory but no money in it. I worried about the older nuns. I was afraid they would have nothing when they retired. I set about trying to fund it.

I also urged that we buy some stock in ITT. In this case not so much to make a good return as to challenge corporate policies that affected social justice issues. The nuns from our other nine provinces liked the idea, too. We got one of our nuns in New York to attend stockholders' meetings. While she was learning a lot at these meetings, the rest of the stockholders and board members were the ones getting the real education.

Some of the best financial planners I know are nuns. They're administrators of hospitals or schools, and have to deal with enormous sums of money successfully. A budget of $100 million a year isn't unusual for some of them. Wall Street could have taken some cues. I know I did, and my budget was only $3 million.

Going over numbers and creating moneymaking avenues was interesting and necessary, but it wasn't how I wanted to put bread on my table. My heart was with people, not with figures. But I remained vice provincial of the Mercys, its treasurer, and legal counsel for several years. I had also opened up a law office in downtown Providence in 1977, specializing in public-interest law. During all of this I shuttled back and forth between Rhode Island and Central America.

Our nuns were missionaries in Belize and Honduras. They were teachers and champions of social justice. Occasionally they got into trouble for their social policies. That's when I was called in to meet with the other side's lawyers.

It was a time of tremendous political unrest. Belize was pulling away from British domination, and internal forces were battling each other to seize control. Some of our nuns were politically involved there and in Honduras, trying to protect the rights of the poor and uneducated. This didn't always sit too well with the official government. So we tried to work out some amicable arrangement that didn't get our nuns slapped in jail, but at the same time did preserve their instincts for justice.

They were some of the most enriching experiences of my life, those visits to lands distant and strange. I had only to open my eyes to the values and cultures of others to see how big the human heart is.

We oftentimes traveled by Jeep. It was the only way to get through to the more remote villages where some of our nuns chose to work. The travel was rough, the climate hot enough to fry tortillas without using a skillet. Color was more vivid, too. Green leaves shimmered, brown earth bubbled. And when marshmallow clouds parted, the sea looked upside down. The people were as astonishing as the scenery. It was their simplicity that touched me the most. It gave me perspective on what living was all about. Whenever thoughts of ego or celebrity creep up,

I am reminded of these sensitive and loving people who accepted me with such warmth and graciousness. They didn't need a report card by which to live life. They had already achieved excellence in values some of us had forgotten, or didn't care enough about to remember. They showed me that life is experienced with open arms, not crossed.

Once I had supper with a very poor family. The mother served me a clear broth to which big chunks of chicken had been added. The family members looked on with pleasure as I took my first spoonful. Then I noticed their soup bowls. They contained broth only, no chicken.

Sister Dianne Carlson had been living in Belize for a while after she left Warwick. It was like old home week seeing her again. She thrived in this environment and was deeply committed to the people. Her hands were even browner than before. She saw me looking at them.

"Before you ask, let me tell you," she joked. "I guess you would have to say that I've learned people are people no matter where you find them. They cry, laugh, hurt, belch, and get angry. The words they use may be different, but the feelings are the same. No one culture has it over anybody else." She shrugged her shoulders. "The richness of life is found in its differences."

"What about their acceptance of their poverty and their own self-imposed limitations as a result? Do you think we in the Church have contributed to that?" I asked. I deliberately deepened my voice and intoned, "Your life is a blank page upon which the will of God is written."

We both laughed lightly, remembering our earlier spirituality. Dianne shook her head. "I believe God keeps pushing the pencil our way for us to write our own destiny, but we keep pushing it back."

"Dear Sister," I said, smiling, "I'm holding a pencil in my hand right now, and I don't ever intend to lose sight of it."

Dianne was right. God gives us the tools to live life, but expects us to use them in our own way. We are all authors and responsible for what we write.

My trips to Central America boosted my desire to effect change. I came back to Providence renewed and imbued with a zest to get the job done. I also longed for my administrative responsibilities to come to an end.

During this period I had been juggling several big environmental cases, including resistance to a plan for building a nuclear power plant in seaside Charlestown, Rhode Island, and a long battle over regulation of the oil-support industry at Quonset Point. I had also become active in cases involving the rights of the handicapped. It was exhausting but exhilarating work.

At one point I had temporarily to run McAuley House in Providence. I peeled potatoes in the morning before court, then returned at noon to help dish up lunch. I attacked the potatoes with such enthusiasm that all that was left by the time they were turned into soup was a watery broth. You could often hear some of the guests at McAuley House ask the nuns in timid voices, hats twisting nervously in their hands, "Who's on today?" When they heard my name, they backed out of there like foxes who had just run into a bloodhound.

Like my mother before me, I didn't do well in the kitchen.

My McAuley House experience proved to be one of the roughest. Those were truly the down and out, people who had nowhere to go, and up was too far away. I remember one time, during the lunch hour, a Vietnam vet sitting by himself. He was thin and unshaven, with constantly darting eyes, the kind you see on a dog when it's been beaten repeatedly by its owner. His green fatigues had turned brown and smelly. He never spoke and others sensed that he didn't want to be spoken to. They left him alone. A plane was passing overhead. It was summer and we were sitting outside. The sound of the jet engines was louder than usual. The vet clapped his hands over his ears. The soup

bowl fell from his hands, splashing the people next to him as he
dove under the nearest table. He crouched under it for the
longest time, shaking. We couldn't coax him out. Some of the
people offered the young man a drink from their brown paper
bags. I didn't like the drinking, but it was their way of life, their
choice, and what was most valuable to them. And here they were
willing to share it with a stranger. Such lessons of life are often
found when you are least looking.

Acts of kindness have a way of lighting up your heart like a
fireworks display on a hot Fourth of July night. Bad acts douse
the lights, leaving everything in inky darkness. I remember a
young girl during my McAuley House days whose life only
seemed to spark the wrong feelings, the dark ones. It started
when the mother stuck her head in the gas oven when she heard
Delores coming home from school. She waited until she heard
her daughter's footsteps outside the door. Then she popped
open the oven door and laid her head inside. Delores thought
her mother had killed herself, but the mother pulled her head
out of the oven, screaming that Delores had driven her to try to
commit suicide. This pattern of mental abuse continued as if
forever, driving the youngster slowly crazy. I had tried to help
Delores. Sometimes we connected, but by then, it was too late.

When she was fourteen, Delores's father died an alcohol-
related death. The mother died soon after. For all practical purposes, Delores was already dead.

She had picked up with a junkie who had force-fed her his little
candy store of treats. Finally, one day, he gave her too much
liquor to wash down the pills. She went berserk. The boyfriend
panicked and tried to shut her up. He kicked and punched her
to silence her, and when that didn't work, he choked her to
death.

The sister called me. I went down to the morgue to identify
the body. I looked at her battered face. There was no promise
of youth there or, for that matter, even innocence. It had all

come and gone too quickly. Despair drew around me like the folds of a heavy coat.

The image of Delores comes to mind often. Now, as then, I have no answers, only questions. If one could pose any solutions, perhaps they would come in the simple act of trying. Just trying to make a better life, just trying to provide those conditions that make it possible.

II
TRUTH OR
CONSEQUENCES

*"Get off my property, little girl, or I'm going to blow you off with
this shotgun!" he bellowed.*

One of the ways to try to better life is to improve the environment in which we live. Such was the case with an individual named Bill Davis. When I was attorney general, we referred to him as "Wild Bill." We were still prosecuting him. But back then he was giving the people of Smithfield, Rhode Island, a sizable headache. Literally. The dumping of hazardous waste was causing a big stink and serious health problems.

Smithfield is a rural community northwest of Providence. There are nice people who live there, unassuming people. They moved there because they wanted to remove themselves from the hassle of living in Providence. Love of quiet and a clean outdoors are important to them. Wild Bill had been earning big bucks at their expense in providing a burial site for hazardous waste. Waste haulers from New Jersey trucked in by-products of manufacturing, solvents from jewelry firms, certain petroleum products, all cancer-causing waste.

The Conservation Law Foundation, which was my first big client as a young lawyer, had underwritten the cost of the Smithfield case. CLF had put me on a monthly retainer to pursue cases with enormous impact on the environment. I soon began to understand the frustrations of average citizens with serious concerns, as these cases could typically run on for years. They involved enormously complex testimony from both the scientific and government communities, not to mention all the red tape that goes with government hearings. The Smithfield residents who went to CLF for help didn't have money, but they did have a lot of interest in putting Mr. Davis out of business.

Wild Bill wasn't put off one bit by our pursuit of him. When you're carrying a shotgun, as he did, it gives you all kinds of authority to make up your own rules. Bill was well armed, and he had also taken it upon himself to make sure that when we went calling, we weren't well received.

I was interested in meeting Mr. Davis right away. I didn't go unprotected. I had a policeman and three other men with me, as well as a court order. As it turned out, the best protection I had was the piece of paper. To its credit, the ink didn't fade and the signatures didn't fall off when Wild Bill pulled out his shotgun. I wish I could say the same about my companions. When we arrived on Davis's property, we were marching straight abreast. But when we got to the gun part, these four husky men mysteriously fell to the wayside, one after the other, as if felled by a fast-moving lethal virus. In the end it was just Wild Bill and me. I felt like Gary Cooper in *High Noon.*

"Look, Mr. Davis, you may have a shotgun and you might even be a good shot, but at some point you're going to run out of bullets, whereas this court order isn't going to run out of anything. It's going to stand on its own in a court of law." I put out my hand holding the preliminary injunction.

"Get off my property, little girl, or I'm going to blow you off with this shotgun!" he bellowed. Then he uttered a few choice words and returned his own hand salute. At least we were communicating.

The next time we got a good look at each other was in a courtroom. He put his children on the stand in his defense. "If I'm such a bad guy," he said, "why would I expose my children to this stuff if it's as dangerous as you say it is? There are no bad smells there. My kids don't smell anything, and neither do I." He folded his arms across his chest and sat down with a big smile.

I cross-examined the children. I was an old science teacher from way back, and even though as a young nun I was usually only a lesson ahead of the children, I hadn't forgotten a word of what I was learning either. It came back with the kind of ease that smoothed my way and ruffled Wild Bill's.

"How old are you?" I asked the youngest child.

"Twelve," she replied.

"You've had some science classes at school, correct?"

"Yes," she mumbled, her eyes shifting to her father's face. He shrugged his shoulders.

"You know that after a while your nose can adjust to bad smells. In other words, you smell them at first but after a while you get used to them, and then pretty soon you don't even know they exist at all. Do you remember that?"

"Yes, I do," she whispered. She didn't dare look at her dad.

"Do you remember such a bad smell in the beginning when they started dumping chemicals at your dad's landfill?"

She hesitated. "Yes, I do." It was almost inaudible, but it was all we needed.

Davis's neighbors helped clinch the rest. One man was a bee-keeper. "All my bees died," he said simply. "My business. There's nothing."

An environmentalist from Brown University testified to the presence of benzine, chloroform, and other toxic chemicals. Additional expert witnesses detailed old aerial maps of Davis's property, which revealed that he had created a dumping operation. It hadn't been there before as a preexisting use of the land.

When Davis wasn't carrying a shotgun, he came armed with his own specialists. I pointed out that they were nothing more than hired guns, who traveled the countryside testifying on behalf of polluters.

We got manifests from truckers who had brought in the hazardous waste materials for dumping. They were accurate and complete descriptions of what was buried at the landfill.

In essence, we buried Davis.

The trial judge found Davis guilty and then really laid down the law. Judge John Bourcier isn't called "Maximum John" for nothing. "This is an outrage!" he declared from the bench. "You've exposed your neighbors to danger and you've ruined the environment!" He ordered Davis to pay the full cost of the cleanup, which came to hundreds of thousands of dollars. In addition he stipulated that the landfill be constantly monitored so that these problems didn't happen again. (Six weeks after I took office as attorney general, on February 20, 1985, Bill Davis was indicted and later convicted on charges of thwarting the monitoring of test wells at the dump site.)

The Davis case put Rhode Island on the environmental road map. The verdict marked the first successful prosecution of illegal hazardous waste dumping in the country and established a national precedent in cases to come.

After I had won the initial case against Davis, everybody started calling me for advice on similar cases. Some of them were town governments that had budgets and could pay a decent fee. I used that money to subsidize the cost of representing other people who had no money. I operated a sliding scale that worked out fairly for everybody.

Even defendants called to get me to represent them. One such call came from Warren Picillo's lawyer. In the western part of the state Picillo owned a pig farm, which was operating much like Davis's landfill.

"Sister Violet," the lawyer said, "I'm representing Warren Picillo and we'd like to have you join us in defending Mr. Picillo."

"Mr. Rogers," I said, "there are two kinds of people in this world. Those who do and those who don't. People who do like a clean environment don't much care for those who don't. People who don't want a clean environment don't like those who do. Your friend belongs to the second group; I belong to the first. You have made your choice concerning legal representation, and I have made mine."

It was during this time that I really began to see what government was and was not doing to protect people and the environment. It was almost as transparent as being able to tell the difference between clean water and dirty simply by looking at it. In some cases, more so.

A group of workers from Electric Boat came to see me one day to complain about health hazards in their workplace. EB is one of the biggest employers in Rhode Island. We're talking major dollars here. The men were concerned because they felt that they had been exposed to some dangerous chemicals and weren't getting any satisfaction from the company. They came to me at considerable risk to themselves. Nobody likes whistle blowers.

"How long has this been going on?" I asked.

"Quite awhile," they said. "Sometimes the fumes make us sick. We don't know what the stuff is exactly, only that we don't feel too good around it."

"Have you been to see the people over at OSHA?"

"Yes, but we keep getting the runaround there."

I picked up the phone and called the state Occupational Safety and Health people.

"Sister Violet," they said, "whatever problems exist over there, if any, come under the jurisdiction of the federal OSHA. It's out of our hands. We don't have anything to do with it."

"We haven't reached that legal principle of jurisdiction yet," I responded. "In the meantime, we've got some people who get sick because nobody wants to stop whatever it is that's making them sick. What do you think we should do about that?"

It's very possible that OSHA locally was right and that it had been a federal matter, but the state representative told me off the record why they hadn't wanted to get involved in the first place to find out who really had jurisdiction.

"If we start poking around and find something there, EB might get upset and move out of the state because we're causing them problems. We can't afford to do that. We need the jobs here."

That reasoning dovetailed perfectly with what I learned when I campaigned for the office of attorney general. Big polluters are also big contributors. Through the tactics of the jobs issue, they keep alive their influence and hold on politicians. The public never really does have a chance.

12
ATTILA
THE NUN

There was a little throat-clearing and some shuffling of feet. The feet are always a dead giveaway. It means you've got them on the run.

I never thought of myself as "Attila the Nun." Somebody else thought that up and the nickname stuck. I took it as a compliment; other lawyers didn't know quite what to make of it. In fact, they didn't know quite what to make of me. After all, I was a woman *and* a nun *and* a lawyer. That was a lot of us in the courtroom at any one time.

Lawyers usually refer to each other as "learned brother." For example, "As my learned brother has told you, ladies and gentlemen." When it came to me, however, they also referred to me as their brother. Frankly, I didn't mind. I called them my sister.

Once I was arguing a case against some high-priced lawyers from out of state. There was a group of them and in order to make things a little easier, the judge asked that for the sake of brevity would we mind if he referred to all of us as gentlemen. I said, "I have no objection if for the sake of brevity you refer to all of us as ladies."

But I got called Attila the Nun when I represented retarded residents at Rhode Island's Center for the Retarded, and the

Rhode Island Association for Retarded Citizens. In 1978, RIARC had begun fighting the governor, the head of Mental Health, Retardation and Hospitals, and the director of the Ladd Center to get living conditions improved at the center, the state institution for the mentally retarded. One woman at the center hadn't had a gynecological examination for years and had finally gotten sick as a result. Patients' teeth had been pulled without Novocain. Worse yet, they had also been denied anesthesia for operations because one doctor there actually believed that if you were mentally retarded, you couldn't possibly feel pain. In reality, the only ones who were anesthetized were the people who had the power to make the improvements. But they were numb with indifference. After two years the problems continued.

If you took a walk through the center in the morning, you found people curled up in fetal positions with sheets thrown over them. Patients had been so drugged they would literally fall to the ground and stay there, or else walk around in a stupor. Blind people sat idly; there was no one to teach them space therapy. Their world became even more unfocused as they slipped into further functional retardation. There were also people placed at Ladd who never should have been there in the first place. They weren't retarded, but thanks to their repressive environment, they became retarded.

I think many of the staff tried to do what they could, but there were too few of them and too many patients. Overcrowding was an enormous problem. Patients took advantage of each other. The strong ones beat the weak ones. They also beat themselves. Smells of old urine permeated the buildings and your sensitivities, and unbearable sounds that reminded you of wild animals howling at night pierced your heart.

It was not a a pleasant experience, being at Ladd. If you were visiting a family member, you never saw where your loved one lived. You only saw where he or she was brought: the nicest, most renovated building. The ones who never got visits didn't have to worry about where they were; it was all the same, seemingly headed for worse.

The out-of-state lawyer RIARC had hired in 1978 hadn't been able to make headway. The RIARC people had deliberately hired somebody outside the system and Rhode Island because they thought a local lawyer might be intimidated by the powers-that-be. They turned to me because I had a reputation for winning cases on behalf of the handicapped. I was invited to meet with the board members of RIARC.

"Gentlemen and gentlewomen," I said, looking at the members of the RIARC board very carefully, "understand something here. I don't go in to lose. I go in to win." I pointed to the large silver cross that was draped around my neck. "Don't let this outfit fool you," I teased. "It may look pretty tame on the outside, but, I guarantee you, it's lined with silver bullets on the inside."

From that day forward I kept my bullets close by. They didn't look lethal, but you sure knew it when you got hit by one. They were made of bits and pieces from the paper trail.

Cases like the Ladd case are extremely difficult to litigate. You are dealing with human beings and their drama, but their lives are wrapped in paper. Without a well-documented case and access to records, you might as well go back to the drawing boards.

Because Ladd Center was a state-regulated institution, I knew where the records were and consequently, in a real sense, where the bodies were buried. In the discovery process preceding trial, I asked for all 732 of the patients' medical files. It was like pulling the other side's teeth without Novocain to get them. It took a long month-and-a-half court battle to obtain the records, but I finally did. The anesthetized were at long last beginning to feel some pain. I also got the patients' day programs, the written plans of what their daytime activities were, and how often they got them. When necessary, I turned to medical experts to advise me.

I carried my Ladd files around with me in brown paper bags. It was a throwback to my McAuley House days. My files fit perfectly, but not with the establishment lawyers. They took one look at me with my brown bags and very quietly, but very decidedly, removed to the other side of the table their beauti-fully handcrafted, Italian leather attaché cases. I guess they were afraid the bags and briefcases would mate.

Our case had come together very nicely. If we had been bowl-ing, you could say we had even picked up the spares. The time had come to sit down with the other side to compare averages.

Meetings with important people are often routine. Changing minds is not, which might help explain why nothing gets done. The cigar smoke gets bluer and the air thicker. The people who don't count still don't because the real players never have to change their seats when the music stops.

I walked into the room and sat down with the governor's representatives and those from Mental Health, Retardation and Hospitals. I looked at them; they looked at me. I smiled; they smiled. That was the nice part. I felt as if I were perched on a Chippendale chair sipping imported tea out of a bone-china cup, which I was going to spill any moment.

I explained to them that there was no justification for mistreat-ment of the people at Ladd. I had the force of good legal argu-ment on my side, plus the spirit of humanitarianism. I also had in attendance with me several of the parents of some of the Ladd patients. In short, I had done my homework; they had not. I argued that what was at stake was people, not pocketbooks. That it was time to loosen the state's purse strings and provide much-needed services. And that it didn't hurt to loosen a little strait-laced bureaucratic thinking as well.

"Gentlemen," I said, "you are decent human beings. So are

the people at the Ladd Center. They feel frustration; you feel frustration. They laugh; you laugh. They cry; you cry." I wasn't too sure about that last one. "You see how much you have in common? What are our real differences? In fact, there are none."

There was a little throat-clearing and some shuffling of the feet. The feet are always a dead giveaway. It means you've got them on the run.

"I can't help feeling," I continued, "that society is measured by how it treats its people." When I had studied this case, it wasn't just legal principle I had looked up. I had taken the time to get a fix on every single person sitting in that room. My research told me that the politicians in the group all wanted plaques honoring them and streets named after them. You don't get those things unless you do something nice for the people, something for which they would like to remember you.

My eyes swept the room once more. "We have a unique opportunity to do for others what they cannot do for themselves." I could see the streetlights go on in their eyes.

In the end the politicians got what they wanted, and we got what we wanted: individual programs and five and a half hours a day of active treatment therapy for the patients. We also unlocked the doors of the institution that had housed so much misery for so long and opened the doors to community service programs. At last, the needs and rights of this helpless group of people were legally recognized. What had appeared to be a dead-end street now had a little drive-through space.

It had been a grueling meeting. I was thrilled at our victory, but humbled at the same time. Humbled not so much because of what I had been able to contribute to these very special people at Ladd, but because of what they had given me. They had offered me a rare look at their suffering and it filled my very soul.

After the meeting one of the RIARC people turned to me and said, "You're a tough lady! I think we've just met Attila the Nun."

I thought that was pretty funny and laughed. Then I forgot all about it. But Rhode Island is a small state. Word gets around fast. Three days later my landlord said, "Good morning, Attila."

13
A MATTER OF CONSCIENCE

I repeated, "Judge, a child is in excruciating pain and may die as a result if his suffering isn't alleviated. We've got to hear this case." I heard my voice becoming louder, sharper.

The judge shook his head and signaled to his clerk that the day's session was over.

The practice of handicapped law was a crucial turning point in my life, and one for which I shall be forever grateful. It brought me face to face with myself. Environmental law was intellectually fatiguing, but handicapped law was emotionally exhausting. It ran the gamut from high to low; there didn't seem to be any middle ground. When you deal with people's lives, there never is.

A federal law had been passed that took effect in 1978 concerning the education of handicapped children. I had joined the Rhode Island Protection and Advocacy System (RIPAS) in March of that year. The director, Peg Tormey, who had worked tirelessly on behalf of the handicapped, and I wanted to make sure that the rights of the handicapped were protected. Talking to the parents of these children made us think they weren't.

Children who suffered a mental or physical impairment were supposed to be mainstreamed into ordinary classes. Despite assurances from the various school departments, it wasn't happening to the extent required by law. When we checked the records of some of these school districts, we found widespread warehousing of these children instead.

Six school districts in particular had made no substantial attempts to implement the federal law. They had made do with the federal and state share for the specialized handicapped programs, but had made no financial commitment of their own. Programs cost money and school officials dragged out having to spend any to meet requirements. They argued that it would be "distressing" to the "normal" students to see a child who was orthopedically handicapped. Apparently it hadn't occurred to them that physical impairments did not necessarily impair the mind.

I was thunderstruck. "Let me get this straight," I said. "You mean to tell me that if two children were of different colors, you wouldn't seat them next to each because it might be too distressing for either of them. This is an argument that used to be used against blacks. What kind of thinking is this in an institution of learning?"

Instead of taking these school districts to court, I had another idea. We proceeded with an administrative complaint with the Rhode Island Department of Education. By getting the Department of Education to investigate the merit of our concerns, we hoped to affect future policy, and to speed up the process of implementation. A lawsuit could take two to three years to get to court. The school districts knew that and relied on being able to settle on the eve of trial, effectively buying more time.

I filed the complaint in August. The Department of Education started its investigation and issued a report in October. The report denied many of our allegations. After our complaint had been filed, the school districts had gone in and literally cleaned up their act to avoid a negative report. I was delighted. We had accomplished what we wanted. Within two months we had successfully pressured the state into forcing the six districts to comply with the federal law. The other school districts saw the handwriting on the wall.

* * *

WORKING FOR valuable goals and seeing them accomplished is enormously satisfying, particularly when they also bring joy to your heart. In the case of little Joseph, it was heartache. Not because we didn't try, but because others didn't.

Joseph was born hydrocephalic. His disorder is referred to mistakenly as "water on the brain." His mother had died in childbirth; Joseph ended up in a state hospital, Zambarano, where profoundly handicapped patients are cared for.

This case had come to the attention of RIPAS through an informant who worked in the hospital's pediatric unit and told us of the suffering that was going on.

"Sister," she said, "please get a hold of this little boy's records. Believe me, I know he is in pain. I see him every day, and although he can't tell me in words, I can see it in his eyes."

A common misperception about these hydrocephalic children is that they can't feel pain, but it was obvious from reading his records that Joseph was suffering from the pressure inside his head. By the time we had heard of him, he was nine years old.

I sat back in my chair and closed my eyes. I tried to identify with what Joseph must have been feeling. You can imagine pain, but you can never really feel what it's like when it's not yours. After a few minutes I opened my eyes. Outrage had replaced my imagined pain.

Two neurosurgeons who had examined Joseph at the hospital's request supported surgery to relieve the pressure in his head, but hadn't pressed the matter. They said the surgery wouldn't allow the child to "live in any useful way"; it would only extend his life. Since he was a ward of the state, the doctors left it up to the administration to decide if it wanted to spend the money for the operation and the extended care of Joseph.

I looked at the report. Another reason for not performing the surgery was the possibility that the head cavity might collapse. But after examination of the details, it was very clear that that wouldn't happen to Joseph.

The case came to court in the summertime. Judge Jacob Alprin had control of the calendar, and it was his responsibility to call the cases to be heard. On that particular day I sat in Judge Alprin's courtroom, waiting for our case to be called. It was only eleven-thirty in the morning, but I was getting anxious. Time was of the essence in seeking a court-ordered operation for Joseph. The court had barely been open two hours when the judge announced from the bench that he was adjourning for the day. I stood up.

"Your Honor," I said, "we've got a case that needs to be heard that really constitutes a matter of life and death. May we please proceed?"

Judge Alprin peered down from his perch. "I believe that I stated that there will be no more cases heard today and that we will resume tomorrow."

I repeated, "Judge, a child is in excruciating pain and may die as a result if his suffering isn't alleviated. We've got to hear this case." I heard my voice becoming louder, sharper.

The judge shook his head and signaled to his clerk that the day's session was over. When he got off the bench, he approached me and tried to ease our exchange by extending his hand in a gesture of friendship. "Sister?" he said, a question in his voice.

I didn't take his hand. Call it what you want: bad manners, insolence, just plain being sore. I honestly would have felt like a hypocrite had I done so. A child lay in extreme misery, and this man who symbolized the fair hand of justice couldn't wait to head for the golf green.

"I'll tell you what," I said dully. "You come back here before day's end to hear this case, and I'll shake your hand then."

There was dead silence. The judge was through for the day.

The case didn't come up the next day, and it never came up before Judge Alprin went on his vacation. When it did make the calendar, we had a new judge.

We also had compelling evidence. I introduced the entire Zambarano record and said, "Your Honor, this record speaks for itself. You will also note in the record the statements of two neurosurgeons supporting surgery for Joseph."

But the judge insisted that he wanted yet a third opinion. Earlier, I had successfully petitioned his court asking that a guardian *ad litem* be appointed for Joseph. This guardian sits in court to listen to the pros and cons on behalf of the incompetent person, then decides on a course of action that's in the person's best interest. The judge directed the guardian *ad litem* to get the third opinion.

But the guardian *ad litem* failed to make an appointment for the remaining opinion. Eventually an opinion was obtained. It stated that not only was Joseph in severe pain and that an operation could be performed, but that it should be performed.

A hearing was set up to decide the issue. A half-hour into it, I received a message. Joseph was dead.

I didn't have a real adult handle on my reactions. I didn't want to feel like an adult. I wanted to throw things and run my car all over Judge Alprin's golf course. Months had poked by while this child lay in agonizing misery. We had failed him.

I called Donna, anger pushing through me like blistering hot steel the moment the furnace door is opened. "What are we really about if we can't help the helpless? You fight, fight, fight, and what comes of it? It's never enough and it's always too late." The steel tasted bitter in my mouth.

I NEVER looked at the courts in the same way again. People are just people and none of us is perfect. Mistakes do occur and, in fact, are frequently made. I certainly have made them in my lifetime. I have tried to be a forgiving person, of myself as well, but what I cannot forgive is the abuse of power that comes from its flagrant misuse.

People are what it's all about: protecting their rights, standing up for their rights, sometimes even crusading for their rights. Such was the Looff carousel case.

If people make the world go around, then the Looff merry-go-round in East Providence wasn't far behind. It was a historic carousel, something the preservationists wanted to keep around for a long time. My parents used to take me over to East Providence when I was a youngster to ride on the magic horses. I loved it as a child and the child in me still loved it as an adult. When a small group of concerned citizens approached me to help them save the carousel from being torn down to make room for a condominium development, I gladly jumped aboard.

Big bucks and big ideas often don't make room for small change and even smaller dreams. When Kelly & Picerne, a very large and important real estate firm in Rhode Island, decided it wanted to buy some property from the city to develop and build executive condominiums, the city of East Providence thought it was a good idea. It could get rid of the park where the carousel was, sell it for excellent money, and still cash in later on property taxes. Big bucks and big ideas had a marriage made in heaven.

But the little people didn't like that. "The city may get a big piece of change, but it's going to also lose a big piece of history. Is that something we can afford?" they asked.

A good question, I thought.

We sued. From a legal standpoint, we had everything going against us. The prevailing theory was that you couldn't stand in the way of big development. Our only option was to concentrate public sentiment behind us and dislodge legal theories ahead of us. The issue became so hot that some of the people on the city council lost their seats when election time rolled around.

But the merry-go-round issue had finally gone round long

enough. We settled out of court. I had shared the dream of the people. Sometimes when you have a dream and that dream is to preserve a little bit of the past because that's what gives you hope for the future, sometimes that's all on which a man or a woman can build a life. Hope doesn't cost anything. It doesn't have a price tag.

In the settlement we got ten acres set aside for a historical site. A massive fund-raising drive was undertaken to restore the carousel in order that the magic horses might toss back their carved and painted heads for all the children to behold.

Being a child has its advantages.

14
LEGAL ETHER

The afternoon before the news conference, the bishop called my law office and told me that he had changed his mind. He asked me to withdraw from the race.

While being a child had its advantages, being a woman didn't. Particularly when it came to running for office. I had toyed with the idea of running for attorney general because of my concern about victims' rights. I felt the agony of the people I represented. I saw a criminal justice system that was basically uncaring. You went to court, expecting your case to be ready, only to be told the defendant couldn't be located. This might happen six or seven times. But victims are real people with real feelings. Some victims of high trauma, such as rape, became embittered because it took forever to go to trial. In the meantime their pain and scarring just continued. They had to live daily with their nightmares. I felt their frustration and I felt their anger. Not only were people victimized by crime, but they were also victimized by the system. That was two in a row, and I didn't like the odds.

In 1981, I got a call from the chairman of the state Republican party, John Holmes. He wanted to meet with me to discuss the possibility of my candidacy for attorney general. My name had come up when key members of the party had met to discuss various candidates.

"Sister Violet," he said, "or is it Attila? I've got a proposition for you. We're looking for someone to run against Dennis Roberts. We think you might be that person. You have an excellent record and have really been making a name for yourself. We'd like you to meet with some of the party faithful."

"Mr. Holmes," I replied, "I will be happy to meet with you, just understand that I have some strong feelings about the office of attorney general and how it should be run." He agreed that was fine and we set a date.

About the only person I knew at the meeting was Congresswoman Claudine Schneider. We had met during our successful joint efforts to put the Charlestown nuclear power plant out of business. Others in the room included Bruce Selya, who was representing Senator John Chafee. Selya is now a federal judge. Some of the people present were the same people to whom I had written to correct various problems. In fairness, it didn't escape them either. Now we were at last face to face, but for very different reasons.

I didn't feel awkward being there, although because I was a nun, my presence was just a little out of the ordinary. The group had also been concerned about that. I would be a woman and a nun running for a "man's" office. But they had invited me anyway.

I shook their hands and sat down. "Thank you for inviting me here. Whatever comes out of this meeting, you can at least be assured of my prayers. However, when you hear what I have to say, you may not want them." They laughed out loud.

I placed my elbows on the table and leaned forward earnestly. "I don't think the office of attorney general should be political. That's been the problem all along. It's the people's office without respect to place in society. It's not a job factory or an employment firm for all the family and friends of the well-connected. The office is there to serve the people of this state in the interest of justice. If you call me up and ask me to take your daughter or son aboard, I won't do it. People will be hired on merit and talent only. Neither will the office be used for vendettas as an

arm of the party. Criminals aren't Republican or Democrat.
They're just criminals. And finally, I'm not answerable to you
and you're not answerable to me. That's my basic position." I
leaned back in my chair and waited.

They nodded their heads in assent.

When I walked to my car, the image of my father filled my
eyes. I was about to set into motion what he had so ardently
believed in: that politics was a springboard for the public good.

I had already spoken to my superiors about the possibility of
running for office before I went to the meeting. No point in
going at all if there had been any resistance. But the Sisters of
Mercy are very forward-thinking. There was no contradiction in
their eyes or opposition in fact. It had to with the fourth vow:
meeting the unmet need.

"It may put us at odds once again with the diocese, the bishop,
and the 'official Church,' but we've been down this road before.
I think we can do it again," my provincial, Mother Noel Blute,
said.

I was profoundly grateful for her words, but I was concerned
about the other nuns. Rhode Island is a largely Democratic state
with a tradition of male domination in positions of power. The
nuns were from mostly blue-collar backgrounds and were Demo-
crats. I didn't think I could totally count on their support. But
I was wrong; they believed in what I was trying to accomplish
and they believed in me. They were an important asset to the
campaign when it got up and running, providing the effort with
a crew of volunteers and warm encouragement. I needed both.

I met with Bishop Louis Gelineau as a courtesy to inform him
of my plans. His secretary must have been confused as to what
office I was seeking. Before I could tell the bishop myself, he
spoke first and told me he had no problem with my running for
secretary of state. "You will make an excellent public official,"
he said. "You have integrity and ability."

"Your Excellency," I said, "excuse me, but I'm running for attorney general against Democrat Dennis Roberts, not against the Republican secretary of state candidate."

The enthusiasm drained from his face as though someone had just pulled the plug on a sinkful of hot water. He even gurgled the same way, his round eyes growing wider. "You mean you want to run against Dennis Roberts? Sister"—he shook his head sadly—"this is an entirely different matter. I'm afraid that I cannot allow this to happen." He stepped over to a shelf of books and pulled one down. It was a book of canon law and he read to me a section discouraging the clergy from running for political office. He closed it solemnly and with finality.

I thought to myself, Suddenly, nuns are clergy. If that's true, then why aren't we ordained? But rather than get into that issue, I emphasized instead the unmet needs of victims of crime, and the necessity of making the office of attorney general nonpolitical.

"Here's what I'll do," he said finally. "When I'm questioned on this, I'll just say that you're a conscientious person and that you have not asked for my permission or my endorsement. You're just following your own conscience."

"I have no problem with that," I replied. "However, I also want to make it clear that I am precisely not seeking your permission or endorsement because the office of attorney general should be free from all political considerations, including religious. There should be no perception that the diocese of Providence is running the office of attorney general."

"Agreed."

Approximately ten days later, I called a news conference to announce formally my intentions. The media had been speculating as to what they were. The afternoon before the news conference, the bishop called my law office and told me that he had changed his mind. He asked me to withdraw from the race.

"We had an understanding, your Excellency. Did my opponent get to you? Or anybody else?"

"Well," Bishop Gelineau said, "he didn't call me, but it's important to look at the big picture and recognize that when you are bishop, as I am, you have enormous responsibilities. Those responsibilities concern the general good. Our works of charity must continue and fund-raising efforts in this direction must not lag."

I had listened quietly, like someone waiting for a ghost to appear in an abandoned house. The bishop's words haunted me. In effect, if I ran, the diocese might not get its usual donations, particularly in light of the fact that the Catholic Charity Fund Appeal was about to get under way. After a moment I replied, "I'm going forward with my announcement tomorrow. Thank you for calling and telling me your new position."

"If you go forward," he said, "I shall have no recourse but to call a press conference of our own denouncing your decision."

I made my announcement seeking the office of attorney general from the home of a victim. It was in a blue-collar neighborhood in Warwick, the kind of neighborhood that is peopled by regular folks who have no bone to pick with their neighbor. People who just want to live in peace and obey the law. Only this family of six had been robbed of their entire possessions. They hadn't had much to begin with and now they had even less. The neighborhood had turned into a high-crime haven.

Poor people and wealthy people alike scurried into the yard. They jostled shoulders with what seemed hundreds of nuns, and the other members of the Republican slate running for office. Some of the well-to-do from Newport and Barrington had parked their shiny new Mercedeses and BMWs in front of the house. Occasionally, the owners of these cars turned 180 degrees to make sure their expensive vehicles were still there. Necks craning, eyes straining, they reminded me of parents looking for a lost child. I had to conceal a smile. They were feeling what victims feel. Terror over their shoulder.

I had a prepared statement that I had already given out to the media. I looked it over once again before I began talking into the microphones. It didn't do any good. I never was much good at speaking from a script. I spoke from my heart instead. "This is a very important day. It marks the beginning of giving back to you what is rightfully yours. Criminals are free to prowl our streets while the wrong people, you, remain behind locked doors. I think it's the duty of the attorney general to return the streets to their rightful owners." There was loud cheering and clapping of hands and stamping of feet. Voices of approval rang the air.

Looking at that throng of expectant faces, I understood for a brief moment what politicians feel in the arena of public acclaim. I liked the feeling. Not for what it could do for me, but for what it made possible to do for others. It made me want to win.

THE DIOCESE made good its threat to hold a news conference at the chancery denouncing my decision. Only Bishop Gelineau didn't speak at it. He had somebody else do it for him.

I was no stranger to controversy in the Church. As a young nun in the early seventies, I had walked in marches and fought on behalf of the poor and downtrodden in positions which were often at variance with the official Church, in this case, the diocese of Providence. We supported the lettuce boycotts in California that had affected laborers nationwide. We got up at five in the morning to protest in front of markets in Providence that sold nonunion lettuce. One was a supplier of lettuce to our convent. I knew that, and as soon as I was spotted, the market knew that, too. The convent didn't eat lettuce for a long time after that. At least, not for free.

Another time I appeared on a panel with two men discussing

the role of women in the Church. One was a theologian from Salve Regina College; the other was a married ex-priest. My being a woman and a nun, it made sense for me to be on the panel. The diocese disagreed. Even though representatives of the diocese had not attended the forum, they denounced me in an editorial as being an advocate of free sex. What, in fact, I had said in response to an audience question about contraception was "If the Church doesn't want to be myopic, then it's going to have to improve its vision. How can a celibate man decide the full nature of sexual relations? You have to include women and married people in any policy decision having to do with contraception. That's the problem with the Church. Neither women nor married people occupy positions of policy influence or responsibility. Until that happens, you will continue to deal with flawed decision-making." That didn't sound like free sex to me.

After that panel and the condemnatory article in the diocesan newspaper, some fifty nuns and priests marched on the newspaper's office in protest of how the panel was treated. Eventually the theologian buckled under pressure, but the married ex-priest and I stuck to our beliefs. When the Mercys tried to get the diocese to listen to a tape recording of the discussion so that it would know exactly what was said, the diocese refused.

The editorial had hit its mark and done considerable damage. People pointed to me and whispered to each other, "She's the one," whenever they saw me in church. I felt that along with my silver cross, I was also wearing the scarlet letter. But instead of feeling shame, I felt only the sting that comes from standing up for that in which you believe.

In 1980, a group of women stood inside the bishop's cathedral protesting the ban on ordination of women in the Church. I was among them. We had worn blue armbands with the inscribed words TRUST IN God. SHE WILL PROVIDE. We stood off to the side so that we wouldn't interfere with the worship of others. The priest denounced us from the pulpit.

"These people are nothing but a nuisance," he hissed. "Much to my disappointment, I see among their numbers some nuns. People who should know better, considering how much the Church has spent on their education. Let it be said, once and for all, the priesthood is for men, not for women."

But it was the Mercys who had paid for my education, not the official Church. And it was the official Church with which I came into conflict. That spread to the talk shows during the campaign when I appeared as a guest, and during debates with my opponent.

"Lady," one caller said, "what's with you and God? Why don't you just stay in the convent where you belong!" I tried to air the issues and why I was running, but they got lost in the emotional rhetoric of religion.

The talk-show hosts for the most part added to the bedlam. In some instances they were as uninformed as the callers and contributed to the overall misinformation that prevented me from saying my piece. I never did acquire the necessary thick skin you're supposed to develop to deflect the hurt, even though it's all part of the territory, and all part of holding public office. It just never felt right.

To BE a successful candidate, you've got to raise money. I entered the race late. It was an uphill battle all the way. I held mostly low-ticket affairs, $15 chicken dinners, the kind of events that my kind of supporters could afford. I once held a $100-per-person event and raised about $10,000, but it never came close to my opponent's fund-raising efforts. Besides coming from a family that was a virtual dynasty in Rhode Island politics as well as independently wealthy, my opponent also had all the union endorsements and was a beneficiary of the powerful Democratic political machine. I raised only about $98,000 compared to Roberts's $300,000.

But lack of money didn't keep me from focusing on public corruption. I thought Roberts was soft on white-collar crime. "The fall from power isn't enough," I said tirelessly in my tours around the state. "Crooked politicians should go to jail as well. All they get now is a slap on the wrist." I pounded away at this theme in my second run for office as well. And when I did get elected, it no longer was a theme. It was a practice of my office to pursue public corruption. The difficulty was in getting the courts and some of the public to take it seriously.

White-collar crime is just like any other crime. Make no mistake about that. But in Rhode Island, the state criminal justice system doesn't know what to do about this kind of crime. Too often the people who commit it are faces the system recognizes: social and professional peers.

IN MY first election I got almost 43 percent of the vote. The momentum clearly shifted toward the end of the campaign. Had there been more time, I very possibly would have won my first time out. When I ran for office in 1984, the facts hadn't changed—nor had my message.

15

PENALTY PLAY

"Wait a minute! You're telling me that no matter what, I can
never return to the order and be a Sister of Mercy?"
She nodded her head slowly and painfully.

Running for public office produces two competing considerations of equal importance: confidence and doubt. Establishing public confidence in your approach to the issues, and doubt in how they've been handled by your opponent. The kind of doubt that forces you to open your mind and examine your own unquestioned acceptance of business as usual. The kind of doubt that makes you want to push for necessary change and stand behind it when it happens.

That is why I believe that although I lost the election in 1982, in a sense I really won. Much of what I talked about and raised as issues in the campaign was adopted by the legislature the following year. My stance on victims' rights, for example, found its way into law. The package wasn't submitted by Roberts, but by a legislator. It didn't make any difference; it's on the books now. But unfortunately there was no translation of those laws to everyday life in the courtroom.

There was something else on the books, too, which did get translated into everyday life. In 1983, the Vatican made it official. If you were a member of the clergy, you were discouraged from holding political or appointed office. But unlike past declarations, which had never stated who had the ultimate authority on these matters, the pope left it up to his individual bishops to make the final decision. If it were for the "common good," the local bishop could use his own discretion and grant an exception. All across the country, bishops had been doing just that. But that approach didn't make it to Providence, Rhode Island. If I made another run for office, the bishop had sent clear and unmistakable signals to my superiors that no exemptions would be forthcoming for me.

I met with my superior, Mother Noel Blute, at the provincialate in Cumberland, scene of so many wonderful memories when I had entered the order. Life was fresh and remarkable then. On most days I still feel that way. But that day was not one of them. I peered up at the trees as I drove through the entrance. The trees arched in prayer over the driveway as usual, and the grounds were crisp and neat like so much lettuce that has been carefully wrapped and stored in the refrigerator. I felt an icebox chill, too. Mother Noel Blute met me at the door and ushered me into her office. She sat down in her padded chair and tried to smile. I was on the edge of mine.

"Sister," she said, "I don't know what your intentions are relative to running again for attorney general, but I think it not only fair but mandatory on my part that I share with you the thinking of Bishop Gelineau. He has made his intentions known that he will not let you run for office again. If you do seek office, you will have to leave the order." She paused, sadness heavy in her eyes. She placed her hands on the desk in front of her and folded them neatly.

"There's something else, too," she said quietly. "If you run, not only will you have to leave the order, but he is refusing to allow you ever to return again." Her eyes misted.

Mine opened wide in shock. "Wait a minute! You're telling me that no matter what, I can never return to the order and be a Sister of Mercy?"

She nodded her head slowly and painfully.

"This is unbelievable!" I sputtered. I could feel a bead of sweat forming on my brow. I hadn't been prepared for this possibility. "Do you realize how many nuns and priests across the country have been allowed to return to their respective orders after they left for various reasons?" My hands started cutting through the air like eggbeaters. I wanted to whip everything in sight. "This is unbelievable," I repeated. My head was pounding. "This really constitutes cruel and unusual punishment!"

I choked. "Well, that's one effective way to keep you from running. Make it impossible to." Tears started running down my face. They were streaming so quickly that they splashed on my hands. Those were shaking. I didn't know whether it was from fury or from heartbreak, but clearly I had been called upon to do some more growing.

Mother Noel was crying, too. She said to me, "You are a well-respected and valuable member of our community. We support you in whatever decision you make. I am sorry that this must be so painful for you." She embraced me. "You have my prayers."

I walked out of the provincialate. It reminded me of another tearful encounter years earlier over yet another bishop. Then I had been threatened with excommunication. I didn't know which was worse.

When you've got one thing on your mind, it tends to stay there, like a rock wedged between two boulders. I felt squeezed. I spent the next months totally preoccupied with weighing the consequences of my decision. Dinner with friends became dinner split three ways. There was them, me, and it. I found myself absentmindedly driving the wrong way on one-way streets. And although I had attached myself to work with all the intensity and zeal of a mountain climber clinging to the side of a cliff, it felt just as precarious.

My friends tried to be helpful. They asked, "What's most

important to you? What does being a nun really mean? Whatever decision you make, is it one you can be proud of? Can you look at yourself in the mirror the next morning?"

One said to me, "There is no such thing as a free lunch. No matter what you do, it's going to cost you. You've got to decide what price you want to pay."

I was grateful for the concern of my friends and the love they showed me. I was touched and honored to be so rich in the one commodity that money can't buy: friendship. Their integrity and honesty provided valuable light in an otherwise dark night. They made themselves available to talk, offered their insights, provided their shoulders on which to lean. But ultimately it was my decision. And I knew where I had to make it. Back at my roots, where I had nurtured my developing spirituality.

I DECIDED to spend a long day in Cumberland, on the grounds of the novitiate. I wanted to feel once again that special presence of God that comes in moments of intense quiet and contemplation. I drove there alone. I got out of my car and walked around the grounds, remembering all the intricate details of the property that I had come to know so well. It brought pleasure to my heart, and memories. It was a cold day deep in December, but the real chill was inside me. It had never left since that day several months earlier when I had first learned of the bishop's intentions. I thought about what had brought me to this spot, why I had wanted to be a nun in the first place. As I toured the grounds, my heart was breaking up inside of me like a ship sinking beneath the waves for the last time. I thought about the idealism of my young-nun days. My fights for justice on the side of the downtrodden and oppressed. How I had struggled with the Church and her bishops, and her repressive policies that served rules better than people. I wondered to myself, Are you just a troublemaker, chasing constant conflict and leaving emotional debris in your wake? Or are you a woman who clings to the spirit of Crucis and not to the spirit of power? I imagined myself in my first habit, the fold of the skirt, and how the veil almost touched the ground behind me. I wanted to weep, but the tears did not come.

I brushed a straggly branch from my path, steady on my course. I had just completed walking around the perimeter. When you give up something, you always get something in return. Sometimes it can be more valuable than what you had in the first place. But you don't know that until after the act is done, and then it may be years before you're even aware of it.

MY MOM hugged me at the door with one of those special squeezes that children get when they're in trouble. "How are you, Arlene?" she said in that way all moms have when they want to know what's eating you up. Only, she knew.

"Not great, Ma," I said. "I made a tough decision, so let's talk about it." My mom and I had frequently discussed my dilemma. We sat down in her living room. It was comfortable, but more important, it was familiar. Pictures of the family lined the tops of bureaus and tables. They stared back as if they were straining to catch our conversation. I wondered how they would feel. Would they approve or disapprove?

"Ma, I've thought long and hard and it keeps coming back the same way. I've always been a risk taker and gambled when I didn't know what the outcome would be. I guess I'd rather be a Sister of Mercy in reality than a Sister of Mercy in name only." My mom was visibly upset. She kept dabbing at her eyes with a handkerchief. Her lips trembled. I reached out and touched her face. I traced the lines that spoke of forgotten youth and old heartache. I smiled gently in our pain. "You cried when I entered and now you're crying because I'm leaving."

My mother pulled me to her breast and rocked me in her arms.

"Are you sure?" she whispered. "I want you to be happy, but I'm just so worried at what you have to give up. Does it have to be this way?" Then she stroked my hair as all mothers do when their child is in pain. In that moment time was suspended in harmony.

By Christmas my entire family knew of my decision. They were quietly shocked. After twenty-three years, you sort of get used to something. Buddy and Alice Ann were supportive. They understood what the decision had cost.

The bishop understood, too. In January he issued a statement saying that he disapproved of my running for office and that he would not grant me a dispensation. The next move was up to me. I didn't want to be released from the vows, yet I was the one who had to write Rome for permission. It all seemed backward.

It wasn't a long letter, but it was to the point. I kept it in my briefcase for a few days before mailing it. Every time I opened my briefcase and saw it lying there, I filled up with tears all over again. A beautiful relationship had broken up. It was like being in love and getting a divorce because the in-laws got in the way.

I mailed the letter. The mailbox swallowed my arm when I opened the lid to drop it in. By March I had received a copy of a form letter addressed to my superiors. I never received a personal reply. My request was granted. I was released from the vows. I felt I had been released from life. I was no longer a Sister of Mercy.

16
MERCY, MERCY

You may wonder if God and I are on speaking terms. Actually, we get along very well. She speaks and I listen, and sometimes we have friendly arguments.

There are a couple of ways of looking at not being a Sister of Mercy any longer. Just because I wasn't didn't mean that mercy didn't abound. It does and gloriously.

I like to think that my decision to leave fit right in with the spirit of the foundress of the order herself. Catherine McAuley never took no for an answer. She stood up to priests and bishops and the official Church whenever it interfered with serving the unmet needs of the people. Ironically, she would no doubt have left herself if in so doing she was meeting the unmet need. She fought with Rome countless times in taking her crusades to the streets. She was a doer. She never let Church policies get in the way of her ministries. The Sisters of Mercy are full of that spirit. They are highly educated, vocal women who have found themselves in the vanguard of the women's movement from time to time. They don't scare off easily and that is the tradition from which I came. They do the right thing, not the easy thing, and they have engaged in more than a few scraps with the official Church.

You have to understand the Mercy mind. It doesn't work like an ordinary mind. It doesn't just get up blindly in the morning and recite some prayers and then go out in the afternoon to do a few good works. It's on overdrive the whole time. Take 1976, for example, when some of the nuns agitated in favor of birth control. They had been around in their various missions and had seen firsthand what poverty can do to people, and the quality of human life that is brought into this world under those conditions, and what happens to women who are worn out from having too many babies. The nuns had already started becoming doctors and nurses and running hospitals and taking care of poor people. Their hospitals made money. The bishops wanted to get a piece of the action, but that's one area where they never did succeed. They weren't meant to. After all, it used to be women's work.

Then in 1982 the abortion question reached a crescendo within the Church. There was much dissension among theologians. The Church was divided. Some of the nuns, including me, didn't follow the road to Rome. But by now this wasn't unusual, women in constant conflict with the male-dominated Holy Mother Church.

You also had that problem when it came to something as simple as running your own show. Rome wanted to do it. Even at our chapter meetings, the equivalent of the annual corporate board meeting where policy is set, there was always somebody from the bishop's office to monitor what the nuns wanted to put into practice. If he didn't like something, it didn't get done. That just didn't make sense: talented women with doctorates not being able to put into motion the spirit of the Mercys.

The Mercys also clashed with Rome on theology, pushing for ordination of women to be priests. As more highly educated women serve in more positions as theology scholars, Rome is going to have a harder time keeping women down on the farm. Women are not subservient. They have important roles to play in critical policy-making areas of the Church. But they haven't made the advances that their counterparts have in the marketplace. Rome is largely a secret affair. It's hard to penetrate those Vatican walls, where popes get elected and bankbooks go unchallenged because nobody reveals where the accounts are. Only a select few are privy to what's going on, and they're not women, and they're not telling.

It's not a case of us against them: It's a case of working together harmoniously where respect and responsibility go hand in hand. That has been the struggle of women in the Church and countless women outside of it. It's a condition not unlike playing with dolls and footballs. The Church has for so long ascribed roles to its various functions and offices that it's forgotten what the grand purpose is. Women who would rise to ranks of political power are an instant threat. After all, it wouldn't be the same ball game. There would have to be different rules and different players, and when you're calling the shots, you don't want to give up the field.

You may wonder if God and I are on speaking terms. Actually, we get along very well. She speaks and I listen, and sometimes we have friendly arguments. The point is, God is not limited, not even by gender. References of "She" should become as equally commonplace as "He," because the point is to be all-encompassing and accepting, not narrowing and limiting.

When I left my order in 1984 never to return, these were the canons of action that strengthened the Mercy mind: a temperament fired by rounds of spirit. There is a gap inside me that shall go forever unfilled, but leaving was a decision I made knowingly. I believed in the ultimate good of it. I have enormous admiration for the Sisters of Mercy. What I left, I also took with me: the spirit of their times. I brought that to the political arena.

17
RIGHT CHURCH, WRONG PEW

He was embarrassed and said, "Look, I'm really sorry I had to do that, but as you know, I'm chairman of the state Democratic party, and, well, I had no choice." He shrugged his shoulders helplessly.

My opponent was still the same, the issues were still the same, and I was still the same, more or less, except that I was no longer a nun. Politically, the consultants had told me the nun issue was now supposed to be a "none" issue. But it didn't go away entirely. It came up subtly throughout the race. The undercurrent was "If she broke her vows, how could she keep her word in office?" Some people just never got beyond that to see the bigger picture. The consultants told me not to worry about them. "You're never going to convince those people anyway," they said. All you could do was try to reach people who still had an open mind.

I announced for office in January. This time, not as in my first campaign, I put an organization into place. People were hired to perform specific tasks. The only person on salary for my first run for office who had any political experience had been the campaign manager. Everybody else had been a volunteer. Many were the parents of handicapped children I had represented, others were nuns, and still others were people from McAuley

House. These supporters helped out with the second effort, too. I loved the continuity of that.

The night I announced my candidacy, a thousand people showed up. For political events in Rhode Island, those are big numbers. It was a warm and friendly crowd. People were there because they genuinely wanted to be. I was profoundly grateful for their support. My fingers tingled from all the good wishes that came bound in what seemed like steelworkers' handshakes. People still called me Sister Violet. Old habits are hard to break. Some probably should be. With a name like Violet, I never questioned the color theme of the campaign. The place had been decorated throughout in purple: purple balloons, purple banners, purple everything except the faces. They sparkled the way the ocean does at high noon.

Men and women grabbed and hugged me as I struggled to get to the podium. I hugged them back. My shoulders ached from people draping their arms around me, holding on to me as if I were a long-lost relative, and then wheeling me around to meet their friends.

The truth was, I really had been hesitant about running again. Two years after my first attempt, I didn't see many of the public getting angry or upset over the treatment of victims, and that in turn upset me. You read about victims of crime practically every day in the newspaper, but nothing happened. No public outcry, no reaction, no anything. It was as though everybody had gone to sleep. So why had I risked everything for what I suspected might be an uncaring public? A good point, one I had gone over very carefully before making the decision to seek office. There was also another truth. How can you hear the answer if you don't ask the question? I had been willing to raise the issue of victims' rights. I thought that maybe then people would listen and care. I knew I had at least to try. It was a gamble. You can't always count on people listening or caring.

* * *

MY OPPONENT was feeling the heat. He knew this was one political battle that could end up costing him very dearly. As heir to the dynasty, he had a lot to lose. When you're in that kind of position, you do what you have to do to make sure you stay number one. Roberts wasn't disappointing. He fought hard.

He cut some television commercials that cut me. They just weren't true. They were also antiwomen. Roberts referred to me as a nice lady, a "social worker," but one without any tough criminal law experience. What he didn't call me, of course, was Attila the Nun, or acknowledge that I had won every trial I had ever had as a public-interest lawyer when Roberts's office was my opponent. I had also argued criminal cases before judges, the toughest jury you could possibly have. The real issue was management, not criminal law experience. Attorneys general rarely try cases during their terms in office. They're supposed to be managing the office. I felt Roberts had fallen down on the job, and cases had fallen through the cracks, victimizing people all over again.

But Roberts got some people who were well known in the community to appear on camera and say the damaging words. One of them was my former boss and former attorney general, who had hired me for his consumer unit. I saw "Julie" Michaelson on the street one day. He was embarrassed and said, "Look, I'm really sorry I had to do that, but as you know, I'm chairman of the state Democratic party, and, well, I had no choice." He shrugged his shoulders helplessly.

I stared at him. "Yes, you did."

We passed on down the street. I never looked back. The blatant dishonesty had hurt me. He knew it was untrue but had gone ahead and done it anyway. To most men it's just business, nothing more. Then they go out and have a beer afterward. It's

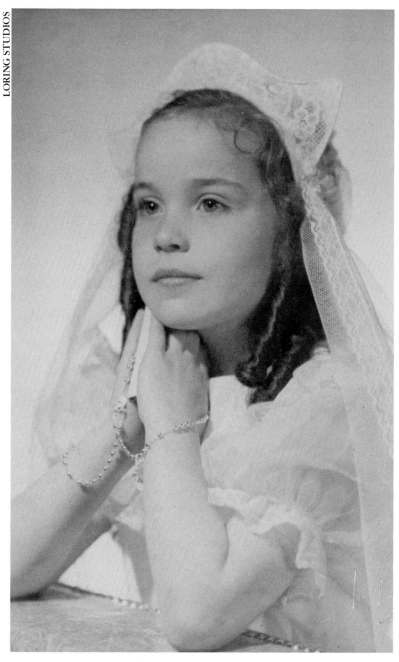

*"Going to church was a visible sign that you were in good graces with
Somebody, or at least trying to be."*

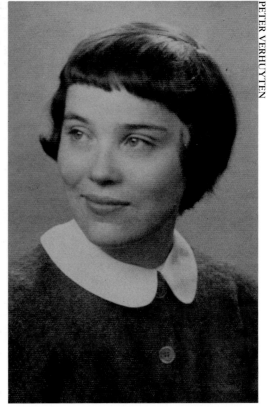

"I laughed, too, because I liked him so much. He was my big brother, after all."

"I finally got my hair chopped off in a pixie in high school, a variation of which I wear today."

"I wanted to nurture my entire being on the cutting edge of a stage."

"My mother always had a fear that I would up and enter the convent someday. She saw it coming in the eighth grade when I went on that retreat in Narragansett. 'Don't let those nuns get their hands on you,' she had warned."

"'Nuns, above all,' she emphasized, 'are not to draw attention to themselves.'"

"I was no stranger to controversy in the Church. As a young nun in the early seventies, I had walked in marches and fought on behalf of the poor and downtrodden, in positions which were often at variance with the 'official Church.'"

"The people still called me Sister Violet. Old habits are hard to break."

"My mom held the Bible when I took the oath of office. I was overcome with profound feelings of humility and gratefulness and a deep desire to perform my responsibilities with every ounce of courage I possessed."

"You couldn't mistake Eleanor. She wore violet suits with big campaign pins stuck all over her lapels, and a straw hat with a bumper sticker plastered across it."

"I said to Mr. Reagan, 'I know your daughter, Nancy, very well.' They were gracious enough not to say anything. It was only later that I realized what I had said."

probably a big flaw of mine that I can't do that. But it's something that I'll have to live with.

It hurt doubly when the media tried to portray me as a liar after I became attorney general, not always by what they said, but by what they didn't say. Just as in confession, there is something called the sin of omission. It has a lot of bearing on your punishment. It also has a lot of bearing on the truth. Every public official at one time or another feels that. I now know why. I just never got over that either. Not telling the whole story or leaving out the context is still dishonesty no matter how you write it, shoot it, or speak it. I don't believe this is a woman's issue, but being a woman might have had something to do with it.

Women still remain among the have-nots, particularly when you're running for an office like attorney general. Proof of that is that there were no women elected to that office in the entire history of the country until November 1984. I know that because I was the first one. When you're a woman, there's a different standard that applies to you from the one that applies to men. The power machine, whether it be government, politics, business, or the media, is basically run by men. There are no women, generally speaking, in decision-making positions. This means you've got to work harder, be tougher, and act more circumspect than a man. If you do, you're not liked and your talents go unrecognized. If you don't, the same thing happens. As attorney general I found that out even though I was the most popular elected public official in the state at one time. But that was the people speaking, not the power brokers. When the power brokers did speak, they set the tone for nearly everybody else.

When you analyze it, both Roberts and I were in tough positions, he because he was a man having to deal with a woman, and I because I was a woman. That part never changed and neither did the politics.

I usually met pretty nice people on the campaign trail. They were a tonic, a piece of the real world. They had legitimate problems and concerns and they told me about them. I felt their pain and it spurred me to work even harder to win the election.

I attended dinners, gave speeches, visited in people's homes. I shook hands at factories, marched in parades, and drove on almost every road in Rhode Island to meet someone, somewhere. But you could always tell the people who really wanted to do something to improve the quality of justice from those who pretended that they did. It reminded me of an old Bob Dylan story I had heard years ago. I used to tell it every chance I got.

Dylan had recorded some songs that weren't written by him. Three mythical kings were beside themselves trying to discover their meaning. They loved the songs. Finally, the three got a hold of someone who could help them. They beseeched the man to reveal the mystery of the lyrics. "We are desperate!" they wailed. "We'll make it worth your while," they pleaded.

The man looked at them skeptically. He noticed that their costly robes bore no traces of dust or grime from their alleged travels far and wide to discover the meaning of the words. "How far into the mystery do you really want to go?"

The three kings bleated, "Just far enough to say we've been there."

ONCE I was on a radio talk show and the caller said in a cutting voice, "Politics is no place for a woman. It's a dirty business and here you are, a former nun. So why do you want to dirty yourself! Don't you know any better?"

"Actually, madam," I replied, "that's precisely why I want to get involved. So that a woman can clean it up."

18
ROLLING THE DICE

I don't believe a politician would have aired those commercials. They were politically too hot. He or she would have turned down the temperature. I turned it up.

Consultants are the new generals on the battlefields of political survival. They pore over statistics and polling data much as a high military command studies maps of foreign troop movements. They look for weaknesses and fatal points of entry. They dream about the spoils of war. They are indispensable in today's political climate.

I watched these advisers orchestrate their savvy at planning sessions. Political consultants think in terms of a first strike, an ultimate delivery system of lethal weapons. I just wanted to make sure it was a fair campaign and that we raised legitimate issues, not personal ones.

But some of the issues we raised got us into a pile of trouble. My advisers had told me that in order to be effective as a candidate, I needed to get the public's attention. We explored the idea of running a series of radio spots that dramatized the plight of victims in very personal terms. The subject matter came from actual criminal cases that had been reported in the media. They were powerful. They put you in the shoes of the victim. Then they held you there, wouldn't let you go no matter how much you squirmed to get away.

Before making the decision to air the commercials, I once again had asked an informal group of people to listen to them. These people occasionally gave me feedback on various projects the campaign considered initiating. I put the tape recorder on the table. Everybody pulled up his and her chair to get closer, ears straining, eyes following the rotating tape intently. The voice of the announcer was low and threatening. He had intended it to be. The musical accompaniment was ominous. Discordant sounds with an unusual tempo electrified your imagination. The spots didn't just rip into your emotional circuits, they took an ax to them.

The last one was the most dramatic. It recounted the death of a four-year-old boy who had been viciously beaten by his mother, and whose body had been hidden under a bed for several weeks before being burned in the woods. He had two small sisters. As a result of a deal cut with the attorney general's office, the mother was serving a brief sentence for manslaughter and was up for parole. Her parental rights had been terminated. The voice on the spot asked you to imagine that you were a little child and what you would feel if you knew Mommy might be coming home. "Home" was not intended literally, but served as an understanding a child could have for what getting out of prison meant.

There was silence after all the spots had played. Everybody looked at everybody else. "Well, I'll tell you. They sure got my attention!" one person said.

"They also made me feel very uncomfortable. Creepy. I'm not sure I like them," another said. "I'd have to hear them again before I could make a final decision."

"But did you feel like a victim?" I asked. "Were you sufficiently upset by these spots to want to do something about the problems of victims?"

The answer to both questions was yes. In the end more people than not felt the commercials should be aired. Some, however, were not so sure.

"I think they're too tough for Rhode Islanders. They will feel how victims feel and they won't like that. I say don't run them. Think of another way of getting your message across."

I went home that night and tossed and turned. The political wizards had said we had to get our message out. There was no doubt about it. It was a tough message. It could backfire. All I could do was run in my mind the pros and cons of placing the commercials like some movie projectionist backing up and forwarding reels of film.

I don't believe a politician would have aired those commercials. They were politically too hot. He or she would have turned down the temperature. I turned it up. We played them and we "paid" for them. The talk-show hosts went wild. Then the rest of the media picked it up. The commercials were severely criticized and the subject of endless debate. Many people liked the spots. They were impressed by the message. Others heard only the disturbing voice: The presentation had gotten in the way. The campaign spun into a downswing. The message was right, but the way we delivered it in Rhode Island was apparently wrong. (When the mother completed her prison term in 1987, she told a reporter that she would be seeing her children. When asked how she knew that she replied that she "just knew.")

JUST DAYS before the election, according to the television polls, I was trailing by some eleven percentage points. This didn't square with our own polling numbers. We showed a dead heat. Then Tuesday rolled around. I did some last-minute campaigning and retired to the Marriott Hotel to await the results. I had taken a private room separate from the block of rooms rented by the Republicans. I had invited several friends to join me.

I changed into my sweatpants and sweatshirt and crawled into bed. I was exhausted, but too anxious to catch any winks. A few would never have been enough anyway. In addition to the TV in the room, we had brought along a portable television to help keep tabs on all three stations. We never shut them off the entire night.

I lay back on the pillows, my mind reviewing the entire campaign in fast forward. Had I traveled to enough shopping malls? Delivered enough speeches? If only there had been more money! I mentally wrung my hands. We had spent every last dollar and then some. It wasn't an enormous debt, but it was a debt. A thousand tiny hammers pounded on the walls of my skull. My eyes hurt. The back of my neck felt like a shaft of steel. Somebody opened a bottle of champagne. The plastic cork momentarily rocketed to the ceiling, then bounced harmlessly to the floor. We all laughed. We had already decided that we were at least going to enjoy the evening. Our eyes turned to the television sets. All the stations competed with one another for early returns and interviews. They recycled political pundits like yesterday's newspapers. They had nothing fresh to say. Then the cameras swept the giant room. The large orchestra assembled on the ballroom floor cranked out familiar tunes, the kind you hear in noisy supper clubs. Excited supporters for various candidates raced back and forth, waving important messages. The anchor people looked like Martians with their elaborate headsets, antennas sticking straight up.

I had been working on some remarks I would inevitably have to make, win or lose. I was preparing two speeches. Suddenly one of my friends shouted, "Arlene, you're in the lead!"

My head snapped up. One of the other stations was reporting similar results. We stared at each other for a full five minutes, eyes unblinking, hearts stopped. I raised my hands to my cheeks. They felt hot. The numbers kept tumbling in. I was still ahead by a very slight margin. It stayed that way all night. I was the projected winner, but it was too close to call.

I hadn't prepared a third speech, what to say if it was a toss-up. People rushed up to me when I arrived in the ballroom and strode to the platform with my family beside me. There was loud cheering and thunderous applause. The place looked like Times Square on New Year's Eve. The TV lights in particular were blinding. You felt bleached by their intensity. People wouldn't stop clapping. They screamed out, "Violet! Violet! Violet!"

IT TOOK until the weekend to settle the election. A group of friends and I stayed at a beach house to await the results. It was bitterly cold, but I loved my solitary walks along the water's edge. Sea gulls squawked at each other as they glided over the tops of waves searching for breakfast. Seashells rolled against each other in a small concert of soft sounds. I wanted to be like one of those little shells and let healing waters wash over me, but the anxiety and tension of waiting for final word had become unbearable. Instead, I just patrolled the beach, like a soldier on duty.

19

BAPTISM OF FIRE

A reporter told me when I took office that I would be judged by the standard of perfection: I wouldn't be allowed to make mistakes. If I did, he told me, I would pay heavily.

When the mail ballots were counted, I had won by five thousand votes. A small margin, but when you think about the odds of ever winning, it was a big victory.

I wanted to plumb the depths; I wanted to scale the heights. I wanted to bring new vision to the office of attorney general. These and other thoughts percolated in my mind as I waited in line to be sworn in with the other state officers. I had compressed all the events surrounding my election onto a sort of mental microfilm that was stored in my brain, but which ran through my heart. I longed for a moment of quiet to review it.

It was a freezing cold day. Rain pelted the sidewalks with horrific force. The elaborately planned swearing-in ceremony slated for outside had been hastily switched to an old auditorium near the Statehouse. It had been magnificent in its day, but was only inches away from the wrecker's ball.

My mom held the Bible when I took the oath of office. I was overcome with profound feelings of humility and gratefulness and a deep desire to perform my responsibilities with every ounce of courage I possessed. But my voice sounded thin to me when I swore, "I do." My friends told me later that my voice actually boomed with such relief and force that people in the audience chuckled.

I WAS itching to sit down at my desk to start work. The Rhode Island attorney general's office is unlike almost all others in the country. In terms of jurisdictions and responsibilities, it's probably the most broad-based of them all. Not only are you like the district attorney and responsible for all the criminal cases, but you also litigate civil cases; argue cases before both the Rhode Island and U.S. supreme courts; perform consumer protection functions; investigate white-collar crimes, including Medicaid fraud; act as counsel to various state agencies, and prosecute them when necessary. You also render opinions when requested by appropriate jurisdictions, decide open meetings and records violations, prosecute certain drunk-driving and related offenses, and conduct programs for first-time offenders. You do it all over again in the juvenile division. In the criminal division alone, some forty prosecutors handle around six thousand cases a year. Ironically, with all those responsibilities, the Suffolk County D.A.'s office in neighboring Massachusetts has more lawyers and not nearly the responsibilities.

When I took office, however, there were a few immediate problems with which I had to contend. Some unidentified staff members from the previous administration had erased some cases from the computer. I was profoundly disappointed in their lack of professionalism. We had to re-create the missing material. These weren't just cases, these were people's lives that had been erased. The painstaking work of collecting information had disappeared with the snap of a finger. This act of vandalism had threatened our responsibilities to the public, but we never publicized it at the time. It had come on the heels of a hard-fought campaign. I wasn't interested in cluttering up the first days in office with the residue of old news. (Although my successor accused my office of throwing files into the basement. They were old files that had been located there since the Roberts days and not generated by my administration.)

Pettiness can cloud your vision, and vision was very important to me in forming the big picture for my staff, particularly my prosecutors. People had advised me to hire from the bottom up. "Clean house and get rid of every last one of them," they had warned about Roberts's people. This provides a certain element of safety. It's one way of ensuring loyalty to your administration without forcing conflicts with the previous one. I listened to what the political experts had to say, but didn't follow their advice. It didn't seem fair to me to fire people just because they had worked for somebody else. Politics had no place in the office or in my decision-making process. I treated those people as professionals and expected the same in return. If you were good at your job, you got to keep it. I was trying to build a strong team with a winning approach, but it took a lot of work to break down entrenched attitudes.

It mostly had to do with politics and judges. The old staff had been used to a political operation and decisions about some cases had been made on that basis.

"General," they said when they got back from court (that's how attorneys general are normally addressed), "Judge So-and-So is sitting on a case where the defendant is his golf partner's son!"

I sat back in my chair and looked at them. "What did you do about that? Did you formally object on the record and ask that the judge step down?"

"Well, no, General, we didn't." If judges ever got questioned, it must have been by their wives or husbands only. It certainly wasn't by prosecutors.

Once I was asked what I wanted to do about a certain politician's son who had been picked up on bribery charges. "What do you mean, what do I want to do about it?" I articulated slowly. Some of the prosecutors didn't understand that this was a very different office of attorney general.

I told my staff publicly and privately, "We have one client here. The people of the State of Rhode Island. That's who our boss is. We have been given a sacred trust to serve the interests of justice and the people. And we're going to do that. We're not going to let people who are supposed to represent the criminal justice system get in the way of accomplishing our goals. Everybody is going to be treated the same around here from now on, including politicians. There's not going to be a separate system of justice for them or their friends."

The prosecutors also told me about all the *ex parte,* or private, meetings the judges had with defense lawyers out of earshot of the prosecutors. This was completely unethical and went to the heart of the rules of fair play. Some of my prosecutors complained to me, but never to the offending judges. I had a tough battle on my hands stiffening the backbones of my own people. Standing up to judges never fully sank in with them. I guess they figured they would still have to deal with judges long after I stopped being attorney general.

Judges wield a lot of power in Rhode Island. As in some other states, they are politically appointed, not elected. They come from a political world and that's how they tend to view the system for the most part: what I can do for you and what you can do for me. There are obviously some excellent jurists in Rhode Island, but excellence is not always in great abundance. Maybe that's why it stands out so much.

Standing up to judges is not new to me. In 1982, I filed a disciplinary complaint with the Commission on Judicial Tenure and Discipline against Judge Robert G. Crouchley. Crouchley is a family-court judge and hears a number of sexual assault cases. He made the statement in the local newspaper that he thought many of the children who were sexually molested actually enjoyed it and, more to the point, wanted it. Victims' organizations and women's groups flew into a rage and demonstrated in front of the courthouse. The judge refused to retract his statements. People called for him to step down. He refused. When nobody else was willing, I filed a complaint. Eventually I received an answer from the commission. It said nothing wrong had been done.

Two years later I filed another disciplinary complaint with the commission against another judge. Superior Court Judge Clifford J. Cawley had run a red light in the middle of the night. The police also said his breath smelled of alcohol. But he wasn't prosecuted. He was a judge. There is something wrong with a system that not only tolerates that but also promotes it. What message does that send to the public?

I never heard from the commission.

When I was attorney general, this same judge, in a judge-decided case (no jury), acquitted a prison guard of murdering an inmate in a game of Russian roulette. Afterward, we went over to the U.S. Attorney's office and gave them our case for prosecution under federal law. The prison guard was convicted.

I never saw my responsibilities as a personal ethical standard I was trying to put in place, but rather as an enforcement of what was already on the books. Sometimes when you try to raise people's consciousness, you yourself become the target. A reporter told me when I took office that I would be judged by the standard of perfection: I wouldn't be allowed to make mistakes. If I did, he told me, I would pay heavily.

WHILE I was attorney general-elect, a newspaper article described associations the chief judge of the Rhode Island Supreme

Court had with known members of organized crime. Judge Joseph Bevilacqua acknowledged his associations and went one further. He even said he was proud of his friendships. He also allegedly accepted goods and services from them. Everybody in the state, including the entire judiciary, and possibly the world by this time, knew about this because everybody had been reading the same articles. Hard as it is to believe, none of the judges on the Rhode Island Supreme Court asked the Commission on Judicial Tenure and Discipline to investigate their brother judge's conduct. And it appeared nobody was going to. As attorney general-elect, I initiated a complaint with the commission. An investigation was eventually launched. When I formally took office, some of my lawyers in the appellate division told me they were upset that I had tackled the Bevilacqua issue. They thought that in retribution the high court might go against them in cases they were arguing before it.

One of the judges sitting on the commission panel hearing the Bevilacqua matter was Judge Corinne Grande. She was also the trial judge in the Von Bülow case. She would tend to the Von Bülow case in the morning and afternoon, and the commission panel at noon, in another courtroom. Providence lawyer John Sheehan was on the Von Bülow defense team. Grande told him privately that he ought to represent Judge Bevilacqua. She said she would try to work out an arrangement with the other judges and panel members calling for Bevilacqua's stepping aside for a few months, but leaving intact his pension benefits.

Now, I love my state, but I began to suspect that even love has its limits. This was incredible. Judge Grande, who was hearing the Von Bülow case, was out drumming up business for one of Von Bülow's lawyers! When I found out about this closed session discussion between the two, I protested it. We had enough problems retrying the Von Bülow case: Witnesses die, memories fade. And second go-arounds are poor odds. Now we had a judge who was openly playing favorites with a lawyer from the other side, and not telling anybody about it.

After a while the commission concluded its hearings and issued a report on Bevilacqua. The judge was given a four-month suspension and allowed to return to the bench. He was close to retirement.

But the matter didn't quite end there. Public debate continued. Impeachment proceedings started up at the Statehouse shortly after Bevilacqua returned to the bench. He later resigned before their conclusion, and kept his pension benefits.

WE HAD a big task on our hands reshaping attitudes and firing up the spirit inside the attorney general's office. Things had been let go for a while. While work was generally at a high level, there was a certain sloppiness in habit and conduct. One of my biggest challenges was getting some of the former Roberts prosecutors to put down their squirt guns and put on shoes. They ran barefoot around the hallways on the second floor where the criminal division is located. They sneaked around corners and blasted each other with their water pistols. It was difficult trying to maintain discipline where none had formerly existed. But I wasn't there to be pals. I was there to work for the people whether the staff liked it or not. Building professionalism was part of the package.

Peg Tormey, who has superb administrative skills as a former executive director of RIPAS, was instrumental in shaping up the second floor. She was the administrator of my criminal division and together we transformed it into a working operation. But it required constant attention.

While the office was computerized, we enhanced our capabilities. We built a computerized case-management system that acted as an electronic reminder to prosecutors not to forget important dates. I didn't want us losing any cases as the previous administration had done because a prosecutor forgot to comply with discovery or a court order. In my two years in office, only one case got thrown out for failure to make a deadline. It happened during my first three weeks as attorney general.

When he realized he was going to miss a deadline, a prosecutor backdated a court-ordered document. Nobody knew what he had done until the defense lawyer in the case caught him. The prosecutor apologized to the judge and I suspended him from his duties for one workweek on the recommendation of the chief of my criminal division, veteran prosecutor Henry Gemma. Gemma was afraid that the troops would be demoralized if I fired the prosecutor, and had argued vehemently on his behalf.

THE TERM of office for state officers is only two years. I felt enormous pressure to move quickly.

20
COOKIN' IN
THE KITCHEN

"General," they cried when they saw me in the hallway, "re-member that case where the stepfather had raped the daughter and the mother didn't want the daughter to testify? Well, we worked with all the individuals and got the mother to come around. The little girl is going to testify and the case is going forward."

Legislation was uppermost in my mind when I took office: writing bills that reflected the needs of victims and getting them passed. I believed that the scales of justice for too long had tipped in favor of the defendant. I wanted to restore balance. Being attorney general gave me a forum to change and improve our laws.

We wrote child sexual-abuse legislation that was passed into law allowing for videotaping or closed-circuit television viewing of the young victim's testimony. Not only are children trauma-tized by the crime committed against them, but they are also traumatized by the system. Courtrooms and procedures are in-timidating to a small child. Everything looks so big. Big tables, big chairs, big people, big black robes. I wanted the criminal justice system to stand in the shoes of the victim and feel how he or she felt. I believed it was up to the system to make the changes, not the other way around. This was no commercial, this was the real thing.

We also pioneered some innovative legislation that required

a speedy trial for younger and older victims of sexual abuse. Speedy trials have always been the right of the defendant, never the right of the victim. For the first time, sensitive victims could now go to court and get their case over with as quickly as possible. A speedy trial improved our prosecution efforts and the victim's therapeutic road to recovery. Child sexual-abuse experts will tell you that victims never fully recover, but we wanted to give them all the help that we could.

Defense lawyers are great at dragging out sexual assault trials. If you are young, say seven years old, at the time of the assault, after court-approved delay upon delay, it might be years before your case ever goes to trial. And it usually was. By that time peer pressure might make you feel too embarrassed to testify, or you just might want to forget about it altogether. The case then falls apart.

The same for the older person. Defense lawyers want to put off trials. They count on you forgetting. They play on the age factor and a declining memory. "Well, Mrs. Brown," they ask, "what did you have for breakfast this morning? Oh, can't remember? Well, how about last night? What did you have for dinner? Still can't remember? Mrs. Brown, if you can't remember a few simple things like what you ate, how can you possibly remember who you think assaulted you three years ago, and expect the jury to believe you?" My office didn't want that to happen. Older people don't deserve any indignities in their lives, particularly those kinds. Apparently people in other states felt that way, too. We got calls from around the country wanting to know how this novel legislation worked.

We also got passed into law a provision that allows a judge in adult court to call up for sentencing purposes the juvenile record of the man or woman who appears in adult court for the first time. These individuals used to be treated as first-time offenders. All they usually received was a slap on the wrist. It wasn't right or fair to the victims. Our law meant stiffer sentences.

A young career criminal I know found out about our law the hard way. He's serving sixty years at the Adult Correctional Institutions in Cranston, Rhode Island. By the time this juvenile had turned seventeen years old, he had been arrested for more than fifty offenses. Then he got caught once too often and was waived over to adult court and convicted. His was the first case to which we applied our new law allowing judges to consider the juvenile record for sentencing. You might think that sixty years is too much. People have told me so. But I always asked them, "You've met me, but did you ever meet his victims?" Nobody ever had a really good answer for that.

I remember sitting at my desk late one afternoon after the passage of my legislation. Someone with an appointment was late in arriving. I settled into my high-backed swivel chair and luxuriated in a five-minute breather. I clasped my hands around the back of my neck and looked at the ceiling. It was like seeing the ground floor of heaven. I felt in total harmony with what I was doing and the goals of my life when I used to be a nun. The reality of helping people far outweighed the image of being a nun.

While legislation was one way of addressing the needs of victims, direct action was another. I set up a full victim/witness assistance program in the office to meet the needs of victims and witnesses of traumatic crimes. It was a model unit that other states followed. Victim/witness assistants held the victim's hand through the entire legal process, from the time of grand jury, trial and sentencing, and ultimately to the appeal level at the Supreme Court. My predecessor had assigned one person only to victim/witness. I cut my executive assistant's staff to one in order to add five victim/witness assistants, sort of like robbing Peter to pay Paul. Those five executive staff positions had formerly served a press function. Unlike the private sector, where if you're cash rich you can hire whom and what you need, a state agency has to work strictly within a budget and a prescribed number of positions. I just placed people where they could be most effective.

The victim/witness professionals unselfishly devoted many hours beyond office time helping victims. Volunteers from the community helped the victim/witness staff. We also computerized the unit so that we could provide maximum service rapidly and efficiently. But it was tough and emotionally exhausting work for the staff. Their faces were like newspapers. All the news was there to read, both good and bad.

One time we had an especially difficult case involving a brutal sexual assault on a young girl. "General," they cried when they saw me in the hallway, "remember that case where the stepfather had raped the daughter and the mother didn't want the daughter to testify? Well, we worked with all the individuals and got the mother to come around. The little girl is going to testify and the case is going forward." I loved this unit. It was the heart and guts of my operation. It symbolized our effort.

If the victim/witness unit was a symbol, then the appellate division was a gem. Before I left office, it was rated the number-one state appellate division in the country. At one point, in a very rapid period of time, we had five cases go up before the U.S. Supreme Court for argument. First of all, having any cases go up to that particular court was an honor, but five were unheard of. It attested to the quality of our legal staff.

Some of my peers from across the country, other attorneys general, had suggested that I leave my staff at home and make it "my occasion" in Washington. I assisted my lawyers as cocounsel. I wanted them to have the experience of stepping into those hallowed halls so that they could tell their grandchildren what it was like. It was their limelight; I wanted them to bask in it. It was the same way at news conferences in my office. I frequently had the prosecutors or other members of the law enforcement community in attendance to share the recognition.

The appellate division lawyers had prepared their cases well.

All the arguments concerned precedent-setting law enforcement issues. We won four of our arguments before the high court. I was very proud of that record. For a little state, we achieved a big reputation.

And it was spreading. The federal government selected our juvenile prosecution unit and three others as role models for the rest of the country. My people were asked to address a national conference on juvenile career criminals.

The civil division began building its own fire, even keeping the powers-that-be on the hot seat. The Environmental Protection Agency had said it would just as soon bag and bury in plastic containers on the Picillo dump site hazardous waste found there rather than remove it as we had wanted.

The staff was glum. "Can you beat that?" they said, and threw their hands into the air. As far as they were concerned, the matter was closed.

"Sue them," I said. "We're a state and we have standing."

EPA officials were shocked that we filed an action against the agency. I don't think they much liked us after that. Eventually, EPA agreed to remove the hazardous materials.

We went after criminal violators of the environment with purpose and dedication. During my administration we won every hazardous waste case that was undertaken. There were some dozen of them. Polluters even came into our office before we sent their cases to the grand jury in order to plead. Word was on the street that we meant business. The fight had streamed out of them like oil gushing from a big rip in a steel drum.

JUST DAYS after I took office, a federal court decision relating to an abortion issue was handed down. A federal judge had struck down two Rhode Island laws that gave the legislature the right to prevent insurance carriers from providing government-paid abortion coverage to state and municipal employees. His decision was also a case of first impression: It had no legal precedent. Grounds enough for an appeal.

The issue was a political hot potato and inflamed the prolife people. As attorney general, I had a constitutional responsibility to uphold the laws of the state. Failure to do so would be a failure to perform my duties. I was in agony. Defending these particular state laws ran contrary to my personal beliefs. I am prochoice.

The phones started ringing off the hook when the media reported that I had instructed the civil division to appeal the judge's ruling. Women's groups, which had strongly endorsed me in my bid for office—in particular the Women's Campaign Fund, the National Organization for Women, and the Women's Political Caucus—were appalled. My liberal views on women's issues were one reason that I had attracted their support in the first place. A contingent of these various groups asked to meet with me. I felt they deserved an explanation. After our meeting they still weren't particularly happy, but they backed me wholeheartedly when I ran for office again.

We designed a computerized case-tracking system in the civil division that saved the taxpayers almost $1 million in potential claims. We had discovered cases where the other side had sued the state but failed to meet certain court deadlines. We succeeded in getting those cases thrown out.

During the first year of my term, the consumer protection unit returned a record amount to consumers in goods, cash, and services: nearly $2 million. We also cleared the roadways of unethical car dealers who had engaged in odometer tampering. Rhode Island had a national reputation as a hotbed of odometer tampering. Some of these offenders also came into our office in the middle of our investigations in order to plead.

The office of attorney general began to resemble the inner workings of a giant commercial kitchen. Legal broths simmered, investigations boiled, criminal cases cooked. People started pouring out of the woodwork to give us tips on various activities about which they had kept quiet for years. The investigations unit installed a twenty-four-hour hotline to accommodate all the calls. We didn't have enough manpower to do the work, but if we hadn't followed up with at least a preliminary investigation, our sources would have dried up. These good citizens would have concluded that we were all talk and no show. This placed an extraordinary burden on the office to meet the expectations of the public.

I approached various police chiefs and mayors with a unique deal. If they loaned to me for six months some of their officers, my department would train or upgrade their skills in white-collar crime prevention. When the officers returned to their respective police departments, they could install their own white-collar units. The municipal officials enthusiastically agreed to our plan.

One of the assistant attorneys general devised a work-study arrangement with a nearby business school to assist our public corruption cases. Bryant College's best students labored over econometric models that closely related to white-collar crime cases we were investigating. They didn't know what cases we were working on, so we could maintain strict confidentiality, but their assistance accelerated our prosecution efforts. I loved that we were able to use community resources, a college and its students, to fight a community problem: the stealing of your money.

We also pushed neighborhood crime programs, helping the public set them up with their local police departments. I believe that if you're really going to win the war on crime, you've got to get everybody involved, not just the people who wear the badges.

*   *   *

I ALSO become very active in the National Association of Attorneys General. My brother attorneys general appointed me to serve on several committees, including the Executive Working Group, a team of high-powered prosecutors from the federal side and district attorney system. We set policy and defined goals that we shared. I sat on the environmental committee, was NAAG liaison to the American Bar Association's criminal committee, and chaired the NAAG drug committee, working with the federal government, including President Reagan, on this country's drug problem. It was a unique opportunity to see the issue from the topside down and to shape policy and procedure that we hoped the various states would implement. I brought back to Rhode Island a kindergarten-through-high-school drug education program, and worked with the governor's office to get it working in the schools. Prevention is as important as prosecution. We applied both.

My administration was the first in the state to use the drug forfeiture fund for the benefit of local law-enforcement agencies. Fashioned on a similar federal provision, we took the assets from drug busts and converted them to law enforcement use. It delighted me to use the drug dealers' own tools to put them away. And we did it every opportunity we got. We even got a constitutional amendment passed that denied bail to serious drug dealers and took them off the streets.

I'M A great believer in interagency cooperation. I don't see that drugs or organized crime—or other crimes, for that matter—should be subject to territorial disputes. Save that for the anthropologists. If the federal people have better laws under which to prosecute certain crimes, when possible kick the case over to them. If the state can do a better job, then send it our way.

Interagency cooperation had been talked about in Rhode Island, but never really practiced. I don't know if being a woman had anything to do with it, I just know we did it. Together, working with various law-enforcement agencies, we broke up major drug rings dealing in multimillion-dollar operations, and got jail sentences for the ringleaders. My office also convicted and sent to jail for forty-two years the organized-crime kingpin of drug traffic in Rhode Island.

I met on a regularly scheduled basis with the local police chiefs, state police, and federal law-enforcement officials. They didn't know how to take me at first. But then I had been through that before.

At our first meeting there was a little polite coughing and uneasy scraping of chairs. This had been a man's world. The brass on the coats and braid on the hats attested eloquently to that. Suddenly a woman was sitting with them, and an ex-nun to boot. That tended to put a crimp in anybody's style. But I enjoyed working with these professional men. Their dedication and law enforcement skills impressed me. By the second and third meetings I felt right at home. That's when they started hugging and kissing me at the door. As one police chief said to me, "I've never kissed an attorney general before."

21
PLAYING WITH FIRE

*In Rhode Island the prevailing theory is that it's okay to steal
from the public till as long as you don't steal too much. Greed
is what seems to bother people, not the underlying crime.*

When I ran for office, I talked about cleaning up Rhode
Island's image. Every time I traveled out of state and told people
where I was from, they always threw back their heads and
laughed and said, "You mean that corrupt place? That Mafia
place?" It hurt. That was my state they were talking about,
where I had been born and raised. When I went around Rhode
Island campaigning for attorney general, I told the people
what others outside our state thought of us, and how many
business people said they would never come here because of
our image.

I thought the office of attorney general could make a real
difference in changing perceptions both inside and outside the
state. I had targeted public corruption and organized crime as
priorities before I took office. In Rhode Island the prevailing
theory is that it's okay to steal from the public till as long as you
don't steal too much. Greed is what seems to bother people, not
the underlying crime. I wanted to sensitize Rhode Islanders into
being offended by *any* stealing from the public purse. It was like
trying to perform a sixties-style consciousness raising while in the

eighties. I pushed for jail, and in some cases managed to get prison sentences, the first time this had occurred in recent Rhode Island memory.

I also assigned two prosecutors to a special organized-crime unit. Dealing with informants was like walking through a hazardous waste site without protective boots. You were exposed to just about everything. Informants weren't schoolteachers, nurses, or preachers. They were just like the people you were trying to put away. Only their deal had gone sour and that was why they were willing to talk to you. They hoped yours was better.

I occasionally met with some of these informants myself. One in particular, knowing my former background as a nun, tried to do a con job on me. "I want to tell you," the mobster wheedled and whined, "that I have really found God in my life. I mean it, I'm a changed man. If you'll just give me a chance, I'll show you that."

I stared at him with a look that could have eaten through concrete. "Look, Mr. X, let's be perfectly clear about your situation. You're a murderer and a robber. You hurt people, you don't help them. I don't particularly like you and I certainly don't like what you represent. I want your cooperation, but on our terms, not yours. Understand?" I stood up to go. You looked into those eyes and you saw no redemption there. They were cold, hard, and mean. Talking to a former nun wasn't going to change that.

Mr. X looked up at me and spat out in disgust, "And I thought you were a Sister of Mercy!"

Tackling organized crime was no easy matter. Prosecuting it was even tougher. But before I left office, we had almost wiped out the Mob's middle management in Rhode Island.

One murder case went back eleven years. Some mobsters

informed on John Chakouian, and he was charged with the murder of Dickie Callei, another organized-crime figure. Now a lot of people might ask, Who cares? They're both mobsters, right? And it happened eleven years ago. So why pursue it?

We brought the case to trial. We believed the evidence was there to convict. Some people thought trying an eleven-year-old murder case was politically unwise. It was an election year, and the Chakouian case was headline material. An acquittal would have looked bad.

Average people sit on juries: housewives, businessmen, working people. A big problem in any trial is finding a good jury. But it's an even bigger problem in an organized-crime case: seating people who won't be intimidated, and who can weave their way through a tangle of deceptions. Neither is easy. Particularly when the state's witnesses are also murderers and robbers. But the prosecutors put on the best case they knew how. The jury believed our witnesses. Chakouian was convicted of first-degree murder and given a mandatory life sentence at the Adult Correctional Institutions.

While I was attorney general-elect, I was asked about organized crime. Who was its leader in Rhode Island, and why wasn't that individual behind bars? I had not been privy to any intelligence briefings on organized crime yet and neither would I until I took office, but law enforcement officials had publicly identified Raymond Patriarca, Jr., as the undisputed head of organized crime in New England. I told reporters that they should ask me in a year's time what I had done on the organized-crime front, including Patriarca, Jr., and hold me accountable then. My remarks, however, were widely interpreted that I would have Patriarca, Jr., behind bars in a year's time. Patriarca must have gotten a chuckle out of that, too. The state police occasionally questioned Patriarca. He always sent his regards. "Tell Sister Violet I respect her," he said. "She goes after the pinstripes."

Organized crime's top leaders are insulated by layers and layers of protection. Getting through them takes years of painstaking work, like putting together an intricate puzzle. You know what it's supposed to look like from the picture on the box, but getting the pieces to fit is a different matter. We worked hard and convicted a number of organized-crime figures, including a top lieutenant, Rudolph Sciarra. He received fifteen years for his part in helping to kill Raymond "Baby" Curcio. We also convicted two other mobsters on murder charges. And when defense lawyers for three mob enforcers tried to get their clients' verdicts overturned, we stopped them at the U.S. Supreme Court.

I NEVER got death threats from organized crime, but I did from others. They continued throughout my administration. I can't tell you what a feeling that was, having to look over your shoulder to see who was standing there. It was like wondering if the scaffolding on which you were walking would support your weight. Put one more foot out and see what happens. Actually, I was more concerned about my family and the people close to me in my administration, that they might be "taken out" as a warning. After a while you got used to guns and bodyguards. They became as common in your life as a toothbrush and toothpaste. But living with threats sure changed how you got into your car, rode the elevator, or walked across the street. You didn't take any of it for granted anymore.

I WAS vitally interested in keeping alive that special dimension of trust prosecutors are supposed to have with the public. I informed my people of the names of certain restaurants that were either under surveillance or were locations of undercover operations, such as drug deals. The names of the establishments changed with the operation. As an internal policy, for prosecutors only, I had advised them to avoid these eating and drinking places. If they frequented them, they could inadvertently slap a police officer on the back who, unbeknown to them, was working an undercover operation. Not only could they blow the officer's cover and the operation, but they could also jeopardize his or her life. Additionally, because Rhode Island is such a small state, everybody knows everybody else. I didn't want the lawyers in a friendly environment rubbing shoulders with the people they would be prosecuting. I wanted an arm's-length relationship between law enforcement and lawbreakers. The public, at a minimum, deserved that.

Then the media learned of my policy. They reported that some of the surveillance operations concerned organized crime. Owners of Italian restaurants thought that because organized crime had been mentioned, the off-limits restaurants had to be Italian. They flew into a rage, thinking I had maligned Italians, and demanded to know the names of the restaurants. Some Italian restaurant owners claimed they had lost business because nobody was eating in their establishments. Certain legislators demanded an investigation of my office in order to "ensure the public safety."

The names of the restaurants, of course, were never revealed. The majority of restaurants on the list didn't even serve Italian food, but I sure did become popular when I showed up for lunch or dinner. I was never asked to give the blessing; my appearance seemed to mark it.

Once I let slip the name of one of the restaurants. It was the legislators' dining room at the Statehouse. "I'm not too sure about that one," I said with a laugh.

* * *

I MET daily with the prosecutors. I kept them informed and I expected them to keep me informed. The door to my office was open from early in the morning until well after normal working hours. In addition, I met with the twelve assistant attorneys general every Wednesday morning bright and early. They were policy makers. Together we discussed cases, the law, and procedures we wanted to establish. I depended on the staff to alert me if they were having troubles.

I also believed in a team approach. In the criminal division three prosecutors were assigned to a team. Each member acted as a backup to the others. They offered help on case preparation and strategy. I didn't want the new lawyers feeling like they had just put on a pair of new shoes. The more experienced lawyers helped the new ones break them in.

Almost all cases scheduled for trial are settled beforehand. Only about 2 to 3 percent of the six thousand criminal cases we handled a year resulted in actual trials. The rest were settled through plea negotiations. Before I took office, many of the cases settled through plea agreements had been pleaded down from the original charge to the lowest. For example, a rape charge might be reduced to a simple assault. I called that "giving away the candy store." But criminal defense lawyers loved the candy store. They got good deals for their clients. The people who didn't were the victims. How would you feel if you had been raped and the person who did it was allowed to plead to simple assault? Wouldn't you feel cheated? Not only had you been cheated by your assailant, but you had also been cheated by the system.

In serving the interests of justice, lawyers prefer to settle cases rather than go to trial. I believe in the value of plea agreements as long as they reflect the quality of justice. That is, the punishment must fit the crime. When a defendant engages in a plea agreement, he is supposed to get a reward, or "discount," off the time he would normally serve if the case went to trial. The discount is what the system pays for saving the time and expense of a trial. It's usually 25 percent off the time the defendant would serve for the original charge. But in actual practice the defendant usually got the discount off the lowest charge. That wasn't justice; that was its miscarriage.

I discussed with the prosecutors at one of our Wednesday-morning meetings my position on plea agreements. "I want you to fight with me," I urged them. "If there are any blind spots, I want us to see them." I always asked my prosecutors to fight. I didn't want a staff of "yes" people. It took them a little while to get used to that. The old staffers said they had been afraid to speak out.

We looked at the issue carefully. Some prosecutors thought the system might slow down and cause a logjam of court cases. But in the end we applied the principle I was trying to establish.

The public defender's office and members of the criminal defense bar howled in protest. Their sand castle had crumbled. I had made waves and knocked it down. They screamed that the ensuing tide would flood the court system.

I met with the public defender's office and with the presiding judge of the Superior Court, Judge Anthony Giannini. "Look, Mr. Reilly," I said. Bill Reilly headed up the public defender's office. "You're concerned about defendants; I'm concerned about victims. You give me something we can work with that's a realistic offer on the part of your clients, and we'll have something to talk about."

My office prevailed. But later, when the 1986 election rolled around, a large number of criminal defense lawyers contributed to my opponent, people he would have to meet in the courtroom were he elected attorney general.

THE PROSECUTORS became more victim-sensitive. Seeing something with new eyes is never easy. It takes vision. You only get that over time, and not without pain.

22
INTO THE FIRE

*We convicted a number of policemen during my administration.
We also convicted some priests. This was particularly tough for
me. I had worked with some very gifted priests during my years
as a nun.*

There was a lot of satisfaction in my job, but there was also a
lot of pain. When you had to prosecute people you ordinarily respected, police and priests, it hurt. Somehow you never thought
that people who were protectors of your life and property, and
protectors of your faith, would end up doing bad things. But
some of them did, and it was my sad duty to bring them to justice.

Most people weren't used to seeing the hand of justice applied
evenly. It provoked controversy. Some in the law enforcement
community thought I was trying to bring down their brother
officers. Those in the Catholic community thought I was trying
to string up their favorite priests.

I grew up admiring cops. After all, at one time I had wanted
to be one. Then I got the opportunity as attorney general to work
with police both as a group and one on one. It was a privilege.
They are fine men and women who put their lives on the line day
in and day out for the people of my state. I love their gutsiness
and no-nonsense approach to making our streets safer. But occasionally some of them slipped. You always wanted to be able to
look the other way when that happened. But I couldn't and
didn't.

The spotlight on justice had swung to me. Sometimes I went

home at night and fell into the chair exhausted. I wasn't physically tired; I was emotionally drained. It didn't seem that my message was getting through.

Some to whom the message hadn't gotten through sat on the Glocester town council. The grand jury had been looking at their police chief and his lieutenant on possible charges of obstructing justice and conspiracy in the alleged false arrest and beating of a burglary suspect. One of our principal witnesses was another Glocester policeman, who was already under indictment on an unrelated matter. Glocester is a small town in the northwestern part of the state, and heavily Republican. The town council president called me from Hawaii while she was there on vacation. "I understand you're bringing this case before a grand jury," she said coldly. "How dare you do it at all, but particularly while I'm out of town."

I wasn't aware of any snowstorms in Hawaii, but the buildup of ice on the line was particularly bad. "As you know," I said, "I cannot confirm what may or may not be before a grand jury. So our conversation in this regard is very limited."

After consideration of the facts the grand jury did indict the two policemen. The council president wrote me a letter. I replied, "I appreciate your feelings and your support of the Chief. I understand your concern that with three men on the force out of commission, it's tantamount to having no police force. But you're concerned for the wrong reasons. We believe a crime has been committed. We're going to bring it to trial for a jury to decide."

We did indeed bring the two men to trial. They were convicted and sentenced to jail.

We also brought charges against another police chief from the town of East Greenwich, a wealthy Republican stronghold. He had illegally wiretapped the private Civil Defense line at work and then tried to cover it up. He was convicted on both counts. We asked for jail, but he was given suspended sentences instead.

The police force was divided in opinion. A policeman's career had gone down the tubes, and it was an unsettling feeling.

I remember later reading an article on the chief. He was a twenty-year veteran of the police force in East Greenwich. He said his goal had been to make himself "the best possible policeman." I was sitting at my desk in the office at the time. My training as a nun had steeled me for breakage of the heart, but it was something I never got used to. I put the paper down and cupped my hands under my chin. I rested my head. It felt almost as heavy as my heart. There was no doubt that he had meant every word of what he had said.

We convicted a number of policemen during my administration. We also convicted some priests. This was particularly tough for me. I had worked with some very gifted priests during my years as a nun. Priests were supposed to be holy men and dedicated to God. Instead, some of them stood accused of sexual crimes against children. During my administration we indicted and convicted several priests. They were all from different parts of the state and all but one were accused of unrelated sexual crimes. One priest was indicted for perjury in connection with the Von Bülow case. My successor in office dropped the charge against him.

Child sexual abuse is pervasive. The statistics are overwhelming. It is known as a secret crime. You never talked about it and you certainly never talked about it in connection with a priest. Who would believe you? Wasn't this God's holy representative? Everyone had turned a blind eye to these kinds of crimes by priests for so long that victims didn't have confidence in the system. And they certainly didn't have it in the Church. In some instances these crimes for which priests had been indicted had been going on for years, and the Church had ignored the problem. Sometimes the Church simply shipped the priest out of state to a new parish. All that did was give an old threat to a new group of victims. I saw it in the faces of the victims, and I saw it in the faces of other family members. It was the ultimate con job: priests betraying the trust and innocence of vulnerable children.

I like to think that when I took office, people had confidence that they would get their day in court and that's why they started reporting these types of abuses. But I can't make that claim. Creative work by professionals in the area of child sexual abuse began lifting the darkness from this secret terror before I took office. This crime was finally getting the attention it deserved, and people who had held their shame and fear in silence began to come forth to tell us about it.

Two of the priests we had indicted pleaded to their crimes and were sentenced to jail. The judges in their individual cases gave both priests work-release. That meant they stayed out of prison during the day, but returned at night to serve their terms. My office protested this arrangement. In one instance it put one of the priests back into contact with young people where he worked. It didn't make sense to expose the young people or the priest to potential problems. But the court disagreed with us and rejected our argument. As far as I was concerned, therapy wasn't the issue. Justice was.

Another priest was indicted on twenty-six counts of sexual contact with boys. He was in his mid-sixties. Some of his alleged victims were in their twenties by the time they came forward. It had taken them that long. After the priest was indicted, and some of the information became public, many of his parishioners demonstrated, protesting the charges and proclaiming his innocence. They said the Church had been attacked.

I understood the feelings of his supporters. After all, he was their pastor, their spiritual leader, their friend, and it was unthinkable that he had been accused of such crimes. It was enough to shake your very faith. Sadly, for many it did. But I was also reminded of the victims of this crime, what they had to endure by way of public wrath for their bravery in coming forward, and of the Church that had apparently raised not one finger to alert other people.

The priest pleaded to the charges, but we objected to the prison work-release program given by the judge. Some of the parents of the victims filed a $14 million civil suit against the diocese of Providence, claiming that the Church should have done something about this priest a long time ago.

CHILD SEXUAL abuse was a priority in my administration. We convicted nearly all the defendants in those cases. Some of them were sentenced to life for their crimes against children. I also set up a blue-ribbon commission to study the effectiveness of child abuse laws. It made a number of recommendations to improve our system. The results of the report didn't make the issue go away, but it gave us some tools to fight the problem.

23
DOUBLE THE ODDS

"Ladies and gentlemen," I said, "I will be brief. After careful study of the record and the facts, we believe that the evidence, if believed by a jury, would result in the conviction of Claus von Bülow. Therefore we are going forward with the second trial."

Judgment was riding heavy that day when I announced the retrial of Claus von Bülow. Von Bülow was the Newport socialite who had allegedly tried to kill twice with an overdose of insulin his wife, Martha "Sunny" von Bülow, at their Newport mansion during both the 1979 and 1980 Christmas holidays. Von Bülow was a former lawyer for J. Paul Getty in London. He was accustomed to being around wealth. He married into money when he met Sunny. She had it; he didn't. She was an heiress with a stunning apartment in Manhattan and an even more stunning mansion in Newport. They lived a lavish lifestyle and traveled at whim. They also entertained. People loved being around Sunny. "She made you smile," they said. There were also servants, friends, and rumors of a disintegrating marriage. She wasn't talking divorce; he was. Only not to Sunny, but to his lover.

Von Bülow's first trial in 1982 had resulted in his conviction. But the Rhode Island Supreme Court had overturned it on technical grounds. During the 1984 campaign I had urged my opponent, Dennis Roberts, to retry the case, if the evidence was there. Roberts instead took an appeal to the U.S. Supreme Court. When the media asked me about it, I said it was a mistake. It took up valuable time that could have been devoted to readying the case for retrial. "The Supreme Court isn't going to hear this case," I had reasoned. "It has to do with issues of state law. The high court has no jurisdictional interest."

Sure enough, the case was kicked back. Valuable time had been lost. Roberts said he would retry it, but the decision was left to me when I was elected to office.

Right after my election, the media began a blitz of calls asking me what I was going to do about Von Bülow. It was the most pressing issue on the media's mind. They had remembered the first trial and the notoriety it had brought Rhode Island. The attention of the national and international press had also been exciting. I must have gotten an average of ten calls a day every day from reporters locally and from around the country and Europe, wanting to know my decision.

"I'm personally going to conduct a thorough review of the testimony at the first trial and relating evidence, and then I'll let you know," I replied. "I'm not going to speculate on what I may or may not do until I have all the information before me." But the constant parade of phone calls didn't let up until the media were informed of my decision.

I looked at the information, studied the facts, and talked to my prosecutors about the medical evidence. No matter how you sliced it, it still cut the same way: The evidence, if believed by a jury, would result in the conviction of Claus von Bülow. Some people on the street felt differently. "Arlene," they said when our paths crossed, "we don't know what you're going to do about Von Bülow, but let it be. The case could blow up in your face and you're going to be judged on this decision. Don't damage yourself. You'll be politically dead. It's too early in your administration to have that happen."

But then I met other people who said, "You've got to retry this man. He's guilty and you can't walk away from it."

I had to chuckle. It didn't seem to make any difference what I did. I was going to be judged anyway.

* * *

I CALLED in Marc DeSisto, whom Roberts had assigned to the case during the transition of the office, and Henry Gemma, head of my criminal division. If we went forward with the case, these were the prosecutors I would assign to it.

"I want you to go out and contact the state's medical experts from the first trial to find out if anybody has changed his mind about his original testimony, and if so, why," I said. "I want you to treat these interviews as if these doctors are defense witnesses so that we can shoot holes in their medical opinions." There was no doubt in my mind that the success of our case, if we went forward, rose and fell on the medical testimony. Von Bülow had already been convicted once. It was clear that a jury had believed and still could believe the evidence. But second go-arounds were like trying to win the gold at the Olympics twice in a row for the same event. Chances of that happening were more against us than with us.

DeSisto and Gemma conducted a rigorous follow-up. They were not able to shake any of the conclusions of the medical experts they interviewed. They traveled to various parts of the country personally to interview these experts. They reported to me, "These people stand by their earlier statements. We couldn't puncture them. We believe their conclusions as to the presence of insulin on the needle."

By this time I had thoroughly reviewed the transcripts and records of the first trial. The two lawyers looked at me. The final decision was mine.

"All we can do is make a case from the facts. Then it's up to the jury," I said.

The people who sit on juries are not a body of medical experts, and yet they are called upon to render an expert opinion. We call it a verdict. In complex cases like Von Bülow's, I think that's an extraordinary burden to place upon people, and where the jury system breaks down.

After I took office, the media interest had escalated, doubling the number of phone calls we received daily. I decided to hold a news conference in order to treat everybody equally and fairly. I didn't want to hear later that I had played favorites when everybody had been trying to get a beat on the same story.

We held the news conference in the library of the attorney general's office. It was the only place big enough to accommodate the news media. And even then it wasn't big enough. Network correspondents arrived with their cameras, sound equipment, and crews. They vied with each other and the local television reporters for the best places to set up their gear. The print journalists from the local, national, and international publications looked on with amusement. All they had to carry was a pad and pencil. You could emphasize over and over again that no one trial was more important than the next, but ultimately it was the media who made that decision, not you.

Marc and Henry sat with me at a badly scarred wooden table, which is used in the library to stack books. With us sat Lt. Jack Reise of the state police. Reise knew the case inside and out; he had been the chief investigator for the state during the first trial.

Camera lights turned on almost simultaneously as the reporters leaned forward anxiously in their seats to hear every word. The heat from the lights was intense. It was a cold January day in Providence, but the library felt like the inside of a tanning booth.

"Ladies and gentlemen," I said. "I will be brief. After careful study of the record and the facts, we believe that the evidence, if believed by a jury, would result in the conviction of Claus von Bülow. Therefore we are going forward with the second trial."

You could feel tremors of excitement in the room. Reporters murmured and glanced at their colleagues. They licked their lips in anticipation of the choice assignment they would more than likely get. One reporter asked a question about Alan Dershowitz, the Harvard law professor who had been hired by Von Bülow for his defense. Dershowitz had made some unethical characterizations of one of our witnesses, the Von Bülows' maid. He had made the statements on television just before I made my decision to go forward with the trial. I had watched very carefully several reports of Dershowitz's remarks and was stunned that he would not only malign a witness, but completely misrepresent what the Kuh notes contained.

Richard Kuh is a private lawyer who had been hired by Sunny von Bülow's children to gather information about their stepfather's alleged attempts to murder their mother. He had interviewed the maid, Maria Schrallhammer, among others. His notes, which were not given to the defense at the first trial, were silent on the issue of whether Schrallhammer had seen insulin in the "famous" black bag that contained certain medications and which had aroused such controversy at the first trial. (Both the failure to turn over the notes and the search of some of the bag's contents became the technical grounds on which Von Bülow's conviction from his first trial was overturned.) But Dershowitz told the media that in the Kuh notes Maria Schrallhammer had said, "There was no insulin in the black bag." He had also indicated in so many words that Maria Schrallhammer was a little liar. Now mind you, Dershowitz was no neophyte lawyer working on his first case. He has been a longtime favorite of television news shows, on which he continues to appear frequently to offer legal analysis. In the Von Bülow case he played to the media instead of to his ethics as a lawyer. His showman performance was an undeniable violation of Rhode Island legal ethics that prohibit commenting on the character of a witness.

Marc and Henry had been equally incensed. When I was asked at the news conference about the Dershowitz comments, I replied, "We're going to give Mr. Dershowitz the benefit of the doubt that he was unfamiliar with Rhode Island legal practices. But that was his one and only shot. He does it again and we're going to take action to remove him from the case."

Dershowitz charged that I had deliberately created a media event in calling a news conference. He said I was interested in headlines and publicity only. He successfully buffaloed the media. Incredible as it seems, the local news media dutifully called me to ask why I had held a news conference.

VON BÜLOW'S first trial had been held in Newport in a large courtroom. But Judge Giannini decided to move the second trial to Providence. With only one judge assigned to Newport to hear all the cases, just as there had been in Von Bülow's first trial, he had thought the court there would be "overburdened." "Providence makes better sense," he said. "There are many judges here." He called in all the lawyers from both sides to get their thinking on it.

I was opposed to any move. It had to do with Rhode Island statutes on the change of venue, where the crime took place. I was concerned that there was a potential reversible error if the trial was removed from its proper jurisdiction. I also thought the trial belonged in Newport. Judge Albert DeRobbio was the Newport Judge and had a reputation as a wildcat in the courtroom. His calendar moved very quickly. There would be no backlog of cases.

But the defense waived any potential claim to a change of venue, opening the door wide for Giannini. He moved the trial to Providence. As presiding judge it was his decision alone to make. He controlled all court matters.

Unbeknown to me, a major renovation of the Providence courthouse had been scheduled around the time of the trial. Judge Giannini knew that meant scaffolding, workers, and plenty of noise, all of which could be disrupting for the jury hearing the case. When the trial was heard, it had to be reassigned to a different courtroom, one that was older and smaller. As a result, public attendance at the court sessions was even more limited.

Judge DeRobbio had relished the idea of Von Bülow's trial coming to his court. When it didn't, he became angry and frustrated, and preferred to blame me for taking the case away from him. DeRobbio was later reassigned to Providence. Prosecutor after prosecutor told me, "General, he hates you."

Judge Giannini, a Democrat and former state chairman of the Democratic party in Rhode Island, assigned fellow Democrat Judge Corinne Grande to hear the case. The media also reported that the Democratic party had tried to talk Grande into running against me, or for the office of governor.

WE NOW had the full cast of characters for the retrial: the judge and the lawyers. The fourteen-member defense team included New York lawyer Thomas Puccio, Providence lawyer John Sheehan, and Alan Dershowitz. Big bucks had gone into this defense. We had two lawyers.

Many people think the state is "powerful," that it can crush at whim people and big business. Oftentimes the reality is just the opposite. The state doesn't usually have the money to finance the necessary resources: people, and what it takes to get a job done. You have to make do with what you have. What you have is good, but usually not enough. We strained budgets and stretched personnel. Unlike Von Bülow, we had to worry about the price tag.

But word had come to us that the expensive armor that constituted the Von Bülow defense had some deep scratches. The lawyers were fighting with one another. Each had a high-octane reputation and enough fuel to keep his self-esteem running for a long time. Particularly Dershowitz. He had grabbed credit for getting Von Bülow's conviction overturned.

But that just isn't so. The court's decision was not based on his argument. The court had ruled that at one point in the testing of the contents in Von Bülow's black bag there had been an illegal search and seizure. The court said that when Alexander von Auersperg, the son of Sunny von Bülow, as well as a private citizen, found the black bag and gave it to the authorities, that constituted a "private search" and was perfectly legal. However, when the state police kept the black bag in its evidence locker for a few days before sending out to a lab for analysis some pills found in the bag, that constituted a "public search" and required a proper warrant. But the state police had failed to obtain a search warrant.

Prior to turning over the black bag to state police, Von Auersperg had been in contact with Richard Kuh, who had also at one time been a district attorney in New York. Dershowitz argued that since Kuh had been a prosecutor, that constituted a public search. The court soundly rejected Dershowitz's argument.

During the first trial the prosecution had argued that Von Bülow had given Sunny the pills in order to dope her so that he could inject her with insulin. The other contents found in the bag, including a syringe and needles, had not been sent to the lab. The court said these items could be used as evidence in a subsequent trial.

While jealousy and bickering reigned inside the Von Bülow camp, Dershowitz called to arrange a private meeting with me. I refused. If I was going to meet with the defense team, I wanted to meet with all the principals together, in the same room at the same time. I wasn't going to meet on a piecemeal basis only to find out later that a particular lawyer was no longer on the case. It made sense to me, but it didn't make sense to Dershowitz. I was also aware that he liked to use these occasions to write chapters about in his upcoming books. He had turned many of his high-profile cases into books. I had always had ethical problems with what he revealed. The revelations appeared to violate

the attorney-client relationship, which is a privilege in law meant
to encourage full disclosure from the client. The client reveals
information to the lawyer because he or she knows that the
lawyer cannot be forced to tell it, or use it against the client. Yet
Dershowitz reported in his book, for example, that Von Bülow
had contemplated suicide. It appeared that while Von Bülow
took the attorney-client relationship seriously, Dershowitz did
not.

I met with all the defense lawyers in my office to discuss the
case. They shuffled in wearing dark suits, briefcases bulging.
Thomas Puccio was a former prosecutor. I knew he would be a
formidable opponent. He wasn't particularly tall, but he had a
nice even smile and a strong handshake. I had known John
Sheehan from my trial lawyer days. He always had a rumpled
appearance, as if he had thrown his clothes into a corner of the
room instead of hanging them up. His eyes looked sleepy, but
you knew his brain was wide awake. I had never met Alan
Dershowitz before. He was small and wiry and seemed constantly to dance in quick, nervous movements. His energy was
boundless. He also had a quick smile, and was very gregarious.

The defense team tried to convince me that their medical
evidence was so overwhelming that I would just have to drop the
idea of a retrial. I listened attentively. At their conclusion I said,
"Isn't that a factual question? You have evidence, we have evidence, and the jury has to decide which it believes?"

They nodded their heads.

"Well, it seems to me that what we're really talking about is
a credibility issue. And that's what every case is about. Whom do
you believe? That's why we have trials. There are two points of
view. I think the best place to determine that is in the courtroom."

There was silence. Then Dershowitz spoke up. "I want you to
make a public retraction of a statement you made at your news
conference. You said Von Bülow was guilty."

"Mr. Dershowitz," I said with an amused look on my face, "just where did you read, see, or hear that?"

"A headline in the *New York Post.*"

"And," I said, "did you see that stated anywhere else? I assume you familiarized yourself with all the coverage?"

"I'm familiar with all the coverage. The *New York Post* was the only place I saw it stated, but it was stated."

"Then doesn't that tell you something if nobody else reported that? I didn't say Von Bülow was guilty. I said it was up to the jury to decide if he was guilty. I think if you call the reporter at the *New York Post* as I did, he will tell you what he told me. A headline writer got carried away and gave a wrong interpretation."

I was concerned about Dershowitz. Von Bülow had allowed him to release to the news media a number of affidavits that purported to show that Sunny had abused drugs, including alcohol, and had brought on her own problems. The media were full of these stories, as related by such well-known celebrities as Truman Capote. But a woman lay in an irreversible coma, had so for years, and couldn't defend herself.

Lt. Jack Reise did some checking and found that many of the people who had signed those affidavits hadn't even been around when the alleged "drinking and drug" events occurred. Von Bülow himself had stated in sworn depositions that Sunny rarely drank. It was disgusting, and it made me angry. When the second trial was in progress, none of the people who had signed the affidavits testified.

But Dershowitz didn't end it there. He went after Sunny again through the questionable character of one David Marriott, who lived in Rhode Island but traveled in strange circles. Dershowitz flashed sworn statements to the media that Marriott had delivered drugs to Alex von Auersperg intended for Sunny. Dershowitz had built his case in the media that Sunny was a drug user. With the help of Von Bülow, he even found a priest, the Reverend Philip Magaldi of North Providence, to back up Marriott's claims. Magaldi and Marriott signed affidavits attesting to the truthfulness of their statements. Von Bülow had every reason to know these affidavits were false, but had allowed them to go forward anyway. Then, when Marriott's relationship with Claus started going sour, Marriott suddenly turned up on our doorstep to tell the "real" truth. At this point, when he had gotten all the mileage out of the Marriott-Magaldi stories that he was going to get, Dershowitz announced that Marriott wasn't to be trusted. He said Marriott was a shady character and untruthful. He severed his ties with Marriott. This was the same man who earlier had been eagerly spreading Marriott's tales.

Unbeknown to everybody, Marriott had made some secret tapes to prove to us that the whole story about the drug deliveries had been concocted by Claus, Father Magaldi, and himself to help Claus.

We never used Marriott in the retrial. We had refused his request for immunity. But we later indicted Father Magaldi for perjury without giving immunity to Marriott. When Dershowitz gave legal statements in 1986 following the filing of a civil suit against Von Bülow by Sunny's children, he admitted that he always thought Marriott was strange and that he never believed him, and that Marriott had referred to a "three-way relationship" with Von Bülow and Magaldi. Nonetheless, he had gone ahead anyway and used Marriott's character-demolition machinery on Sunny. Dershowitz tried his cases in the media, not in the courts.

But the Von Bülow case had gotten more complicated, and we weren't even into the trial phase yet when Judge Grande knocked the bedrock right out from under us. We were still in pretrial motions. These are little legal battles each side has with the other before the start of the actual trial. They establish the ground rules as to which areas you can and cannot get into. So far the defense had been winning them. Our case kept getting whittled down until it was becoming almost unrecognizable.

What we were able to introduce at the second trial was considerably different from the first. Among the motions filed were those involving the testimony of both Alexandra Isles, Von Bülow's lover, and Morris Gurley, the banker who knew inside out Claus's financial condition and what he stood to gain from the death of Sunny. Judge Grande decided to defer her ruling as to whether that testimony could come in until after she got back from vacation. That was a week before the trial was supposed to start. It was too close for comfort. How were you supposed to prepare your case if you didn't know whether you could establish a motive? Motive was the heartbeat of our case. And Judge Grande had just about stopped us from ticking. Such a ruling affected both the prosecution and the defense in the preparation of their respective cases.

I decided to take on Grande. I publicly disclosed my concern. That made both Marc and Henry very nervous.

"General," they said, "please don't provoke her. It will only antagonize her and make our work tougher."

But our case had been shrinking daily. It had lost its important components as a result of adverse pretrial rulings. "I understand what you're saying, believe me, but I feel strongly we have to take some action to stanch the hemorrhaging," I told Marc and Henry.

Judge Grande did eventually make a ruling allowing some of the love interest as a motive. But she refused to make a ruling on the money motive until the trial was well under way. She had deftly placed us in that proverbial position of being between a rock and a hard place. If I appealed her decision, it would have resulted in an instant delay of the trial. I discussed the appeal issue with Marc and Henry. We reluctantly concluded that we would gain nothing by a delay.

Not knowing whether we would be able to introduce the money motive meant we couldn't talk about it effectively in our opening arguments at the trial. We ended up tiptoeing around it. As a juror, you sort of knew Claus may have had something to gain by attempting to kill his wife. You just didn't know what.

During the trial Judge Grande ruled that the prosecution could not introduce the money motive. It was a stunning blow. If we had been able to talk about money, the jury would have learned that Claus stood to gain $14 million upon his wife's death, and that the first coma occurred fifteen days after Sunny signed a new will leaving that much money to Claus. How could you not possibly consider money a motive in an attempted murder case? Particularly when Claus, according to the banker's records, had earned at the most only $33,000 between 1967 and 1980. And that after 1974 he had listed no income. It was an incredible ruling and it gutted our case. To this day it defies explanation. Judge Grande did not put her reasons on the record, even though she made the ruling in open court. In addition, her ruling was in direct conflict with the ruling of the first trial judge, Judge Thomas Needham, who had allowed the money motive and all the testimony.

With the exception of this ruling, the media had a hard time, for the most part, coming up with interesting tidbits to titillate its various audiences. Aside from describing what Claus and his new lover, Andrea Reynolds, ate for breakfast, lunch, and dinner, and what they wore when they ate breakfast, lunch, and dinner, and what they said when they ate breakfast, lunch, and dinner, the media scrambled for stories. One newspaper, the Providence *Journal-Bulletin,* was reduced to writing about the trial from the perspective of a professional "face reader" from Cranston, Rhode Island. The face reader predicted quite accurately that Claus would be set free. Not as the result of any legal consequences, but because of the shape of his face. Journalism had reached an all-time high.

Radio stations in East Providence and New York played an old 1966 hit, "Sunny," laced with new lyrics: "Sunny, I married you

but I gave you harm. Sunny, I stuck a needle in your arm. . . ."
And so the song went. The media had gotten out of control.

Claus and Andrea, in the meantime, had been wining and dining the media. They took out a different reporter every night. That was the next day's scoop. It worked very well. The reporter got a free meal and an inside story; Claus and Andrea got the pleasure of creating it. Favorable to themselves, of course. The coziness in the end was such that during the reading of the verdict, a local television reporter, Jim Taricani, sat pressed shoulder to shoulder with Andrea and held hands with her. When Claus was acquitted, he clasped her arm in victory; and he got the first interview with the free man. It was a stunning performance all the way around.

MIDWAY THROUGH the trial, Claus's lawyers approached us. They wanted to enter into a plea agreement on behalf of their client. They said Von Bülow wanted to plead guilty to a lesser charge, such as criminal negligence for failing to call a doctor when Sunny went into a coma. That way he wouldn't have to go to jail. And Von Bülow, above all, wanted to avoid going to jail. My gut reaction was no. The punishment didn't fit the crime. I talked it over with Alex von Auersperg and his sister, Annie-Laurie Kneissl, and told them what I thought. They wouldn't hear of it either. Such a plea without jail was odious to them. We rejected the offer.

Claus von Bülow never took the stand in his own defense. The lawyers at the second trial said the lawyers at the first trial had made a mistake by not putting him on. They never put him on either. Nobody ever got to hear Claus under cross-examination.

The jury did not believe the prosecution's medical evidence that the insulin on the needle was the result of Claus von Bülow trying to murder his wife. It believed what the defense argued, that the reading for insulin was a "false positive," that when amobarbital and Valium are present in needle washings, it can sometimes look as if insulin is present as well.

THE TRIAL is over, but the sadness I feel for Sunny von Bülow and her children is not.

Claus von Bülow cannot be tried again for attempted murder. But in the $56 million civil suit filed against Von Bülow by the children, the latest laboratory studies show what the prosecution had argued to the jurors: that the needle contained traces of insulin, amobarbital, and Valium. I quote from a newspaper article: "Further, experiments ruled out the possibility that 'cross-reactivity of other drugs' produced false positive readings for insulin, according to a copy of the lab report obtained by the Journal-Bulletin."

24

GEARING UP
AND BEARING DOWN

A lot had been working through my mind by the time my interview with 60 Minutes *rolled around. The Collins matter had broken. A potentially huge public corruption scandal appeared to be emerging; already its head poked through the ice-capped winter. Other investigations had heated up, and now, worst of all, Morley Safer waited for me down at the end of the hall.*

The idea of a woman being a state attorney general, the first one elected in the history of the country, apparently created quite a media stir. A former staff member had informed us that we should expect just a few phone calls a day from the media. Instead, we answered more than several dozen every day until the end of my administration.

One of those calling was *60 Minutes.* It wanted to do a profile piece. I wasn't interested; I was too involved in my work. I told them, "Thanks, but no thanks."

The producer was very surprised. "I don't think you understand," she said. "This is *60 Minutes* calling."

I thought that was the end of it, but they called again to see if I had reconsidered. I hadn't.

"I can't believe you're turning us down!" came this exasperated voice at the other end of the line. "Nobody turns us down. Look, we just want to talk to you to see if there's really a strong enough reason to do a piece. Can we meet?"

"Sorry," I said. "I appreciate your interest, but I don't think it's going to be possible." My response was just about as final as you could get.

But the producer, Suzanne St. Pierre, phoned again. There was a smile in her voice, but it covered a steel windpipe. "How about if I come up from New York? You take a look at us, we take a look at you. If there's a good reason to do the story, let's talk about it then."

I had said no so many times that I felt like a computer whose memory function had stuck. I decided that a more human dimension was called for. My only free time, given her requirements, was the day that I was scheduled to argue a case before the Rhode Island Supreme Court. I had an hour afterward. She asked if she could attend my oral arguments. I saw no problem, it was a public event, and agreed to meet with her after court.

Whenever it had been possible, I pitched in with the staff and personally handled cases. I worked in rotation with my appellate division. My turn had come up. The case I was to argue involved two policemen who had been charged in a wrongful death suit. They had picked up late at night an elderly man, who had been thoroughly intoxicated and helpless. The man was something of an invalid and used a cane to walk. The policemen took him to the hospital and then afterward dropped him off on a street corner. The man really should have been driven home. It had been a freezing cold night and he was barely conscious. Instead, he lay on the street corner, exposed to the cold, and unable to take care of himself. He died. The two policemen, who had been convicted in the lower court for negligence in their duties, appealed their convictions. I had to argue against them.

Our case was very difficult. I had known going in that our chances of winning were not good. But we had also wanted to establish as a law enforcement tool the legal right to use voice prints. This was the test case. We had alleged that one of the policemen had called his station to tell the officer on duty about the man. Voice prints had confirmed the identity of the caller. I argued before the court that voice print technology had evolved to a highly sophisticated state of science and therefore was very reliable. I was convinced of its importance to law enforcement.

The justices listened carefully and asked some pointed questions. Much later, they rendered a written decision upholding the policemen's appeal. But the court also allowed the use of voice prints in this case and in future cases as a valid law-enforcement tool.

I met with the CBS producer as we had agreed. I guess she felt there was a compelling reason to do a story, and I liked her straightforwardness and journalistic integrity. She had done a thorough background job. I agreed to allow *60 Minutes* to bring its cameras to Rhode Island to interview me.

During this time state police had picked up a drifter by the name of David Roger Collins. His arrest followed a chain of accidental events. A seventeen-year-old boy had been killed when he piled his car into a tree after a high-speed chase. Local police found a name and an address in his pocket. They went to a residence thinking they were notifying a relative. Inside an incredibly filthy apartment police found alone thirteen-year-old Jim Jordan of California. He stood transfixed. He had allegedly been abducted two years earlier by Collins, terrorized, and sexually abused. He had been carted around the country in a fast-moving odyssey, afraid to leave Collins, unwilling to call his parents. The drifter had convinced him that his parents didn't want him.

Police found photos of twenty-five young people in the apartment, some naked, and all believed to have been victims of Collins at one time or another. A massive nationwide effort to identify the photographs was immediately launched. Putting names to faces had been no easy matter. The media helped by running the story on network news and in national and local newspapers. As a result of the coverage and good police work, we learned that Collins had traveled extensively, allegedly victimizing young boys wherever he had gone. It was at once a bizarre and tragic story. A terrible darkness had descended there that literally devoured the light. Families had been destroyed by uncertainty; children, by what they knew. And one man appeared to be the key to it all.

Collins was middle-aged, possessed no remarkable or distinguishing characteristics, and was neither masterful in stance nor magnetic in appearance. You wouldn't look at him twice. But he had somehow cultivated the trust of young boys and used them.

We notified Jim's parents that we had their son. I met with the three of them when they were reunited. The couple had come out from California. Tears of joy and thankfulness sprang to the father's eyes when he grasped his son in his arms. Jim allowed himself to be held, but he was almost shy with his parents. When you had been told over and over that your parents didn't love you, didn't want you, it was kind of hard to believe that they did, even when you saw them standing there. Then Jim started to warm up, and quietly held his mom by her arm.

Jim came back from California a year later to testify against the man he had been forced to call Father. David Roger Collins was convicted and sentenced to a double life sentence plus twenty years.

A LOT had been working through my mind by the time my interview with *60 Minutes* rolled around. The Collins matter had broken. A potentially huge public corruption scandal appeared to be emerging; already its head had poked through the ice-capped winter. Other investigations had heated up, and now, worst of all, Morley Safer waited for me down at the end of the hall. The *60 Minutes* crew had been in town a few days shooting footage in advance of Safer's arrival. I had worn a cordless microphone all day for two days. I tried to remember to be careful about what I was saying; I didn't want to give away any "secrets of state." The film crew tracked with me to hearings on my legislation at the Statehouse, attended dinner speeches, filmed various office activities that wouldn't compromise the confidentiality of my job, and chatted with me in between times. But you always wondered what the recognizable faces of 60 Minutes were really like. Via the medium of television, you saw them so often in your home that they seemed like relatives who came over every Sunday night for a free dinner. And as with relatives, sometimes you liked what they did; other times you didn't.

The 60 Minutes crew worked tirelessly and professionally. In particular, Suzanne St. Pierre was both fair-minded and open-minded, qualities you expect in journalists but rarely find. Fairness is all that you can ever hope for. But sometimes getting it is like praying to a god who has ears stuffed with cotton. Like everything else in life, the quality of journalism depends upon who is practicing it. I think that people should be demanding of their reporters. Journalists like to say that they're acting on behalf of the "public's right to know." But too few reporters are accountable to that public they claim to represent. If they were, the quality of journalism would improve.

My office resembled the waiting room of an airport in a small East African country. The only items missing were goats and squabbling chickens. I don't think I have ever seen so much camera gear in one place at one time as I did that day in mid-March. It came to tons of equipment. Our main elevator had had problems hauling reporters to the third floor in January for the Von Bülow interview. It was nothing compared to what we went through for this. It must have taken a full hour to get the equipment from the first floor to the fifth, and set up. Then it had to be checked out to make sure it was working. That took even more time.

Not only did the 60 Minutes crew place floor lights in strategic locations as if they were chrome sentinels, but they also "pasted" overhead lights to the ceiling, something local television crews didn't do. Slowly the office transformed itself from an airport lounge to a small Cecil B. de Mille sound stage. I became nervous. I began to suspect that this was indeed show biz. A film camera had been positioned behind me to shoot Morley Safer over my shoulder, and another one had been set up in front of me. It had become unbearably hot in the room, and we hadn't even started. The hotter it got, the more nervous I got. Whenever I get that on edge, I hide behind laughter. I tend to think I am Joan Rivers.

Then Morley Safer walked into the room. You almost didn't know it at first. He was of medium height and build and slipped in with everybody else. But the slicked-down wavy hair and the handkerchief in the jacket pocket gave him away, plus the fact that he took the chair across from me. We introduced ourselves, sat back down, and the cameras started rolling.

Safer said, "Here you are, the attorney general of a state which is the most publicly corrupt in the country. You've got a chief justice who has organized-crime figures for friends. Last week *Newsweek* called Rhode Island the cocaine capital from Maine to Miami and the center of organized crime in New England. So, what do you think you can do about it?"

My life passed before my eyes. "Mr. Safer," I replied, "that is the perception and not necessarily the reality. I'm not sure that our organized-crime problem is any worse than anybody else's, or our drug problem. But it's my job to do something about the perception of that. I want to clean up the image here, so that nobody else has to ask that question again."

CBS didn't use that, but I never forgot Safer's words. They had just confirmed my worst fears. On a national scale we had arrived at the bottom. I loved my state, but I also felt a tremendous burden to clean it up as fast as I could.

At another point in the interview he referred to a statement

I had made in 1975 about all politicians being gutless. Safer said, Now that you're a politician, does that still hold?" Suzanne St. Pierre had done a very thorough job.

"From time to time I feel that decisions are not made not because they're the right thing to do, but that it interferes with people's political careers, and that's what I consider gutless," I said evenly.

The interview had the effect of a roller-coaster ride. Safer suddenly shifted gears. He was riding in front and I was getting whiplashed in the back. "Would you consider getting married?"

I ended with, "Is that an offer?"

We both laughed.

"Five years ago in an interview, you said you prayed for an hour each morning. Fine for a lawyer, certainly for a nun. What about an attorney general?"

"Yes, I certainly do. I certainly do. You wouldn't believe the prayers I said prior to your coming in."

DURING THE year following the 60 *Minutes* interview, and throughout my administration, we prosecuted dozens of murder cases and obtained convictions in nearly all of them. A woman who killed her husband for insurance money, two men who beat an eighty-nine-year-old woman to death when they robbed her house, two other men who beat an old man to death when they ransacked his apartment looking for money. It seemed an endless list of murders. For a small state like Rhode Island, it was. It shouldn't have been.

The Jerri Ann Richard murder was probably the most brutal and shocking of all. She was a four-month-old baby who had been raped and then killed. Nothing had been held back from the grand jury investigating the matter. We presented both the good and bad aspects of the evidence. That was the standard we applied to all the cases during my administration. It was a search for the truth. The grand jury voted to indict the baby's mother and father. Ralph Richard was charged with rape and conspiracy, Donna Richard with murder.

Over our objections the trial judge severed the case into two separate trials. We prosecuted Ralph Richard first. He was acquitted. Our theory of the rape and murder was devastated. We needed to convict Ralph on the rape charge in order to establish the murder motive at Donna's trial. Without the rape conviction, we couldn't proceed against Donna successfully. Consequently we never brought her to trial. A trial would more than likely have resulted in an acquittal. A defendant can't be tried twice once he or she has been acquitted. The way it is now, the case remains an open investigation. New charges can be brought anytime the evidence merits them.

But this case eats me up. We did our job bringing it to a jury, and the jury did its. But that's no consolation. While the attorney general cannot be the jury, the judge cannot be the jury, and neither can the lawyers, somewhere, somehow, there has to be justice for Jerri Ann.

I liked my job, but those are the tough moments, the Jerri Ann cases. They emptied you out like a dam whose walls have burst. There is nothing left, just a trickle of what you used to be. You fought against what you felt inside and just worked all that much harder the next time.

NOT EVERYBODY I met was in a courtroom. From people in the street to the nation's top leaders in government, a number of people touched my life in some way. I received numerous invitations from around the country to speak, attended special functions, and accepted local and national awards. Those occasions broke into my work like rare paths of sunshine splitting a dead gray forest. I needed them. They were welcome respites from constantly tending the battle zone.

On one such occasion I had been invited to Washington to attend a state dinner the President was hosting. I was escorted to the event by a very handsome Coast Guard officer. When we entered one of those famous rooms at the White House where a cocktail reception was in progress, I was the first person the President's daughter, Maureen Reagan, saw. I had met Maureen a number of times at events for women political candidates. She hugged me warmly and we chatted. My escort and I then circled the room and just happened to be standing at the doorway when Vice President Bush arrived. I was the first person he greeted. Then Attorney General Meese followed and shook my hand. I navigated the room once more and was just coming around to the entrance when President and Mrs. Reagan spotted me first and began chatting. By this time some among the Washington set had begun to wonder if I were co-hosting the affair. I could hear buzzing and whispers. "Who is that person?" People slithered up to me for a closer look. It was one of those rare moments in life when you somehow ended up being in the right place at the right time, and then didn't know what to do about it.

Dinner was announced and we moved into a large dining area. I was seated at President Reagan's table. The other guests included Joe Namath, the author John Irving, the Algerian president's wife, and "Bloom County" cartoonist Berke Breathed. Later Namath asked me to dance. He was very warm and funny. The following day one of the Washington papers stated that Namath had abandoned his pregnant wife, who had also attended the dinner, in order to dance with me. It had been unfortunate that Namath hadn't carried insurance on his feet. He could have collected a hefty sum from me. One dance had been enough.

At one point in the evening I found myself alone with both the President and Nancy Reagan. I said to Mr. Reagan, "I know your daughter, Nancy, very well." They were gracious enough not to say anything. It was only later I realized what I had said. In rebuttal of something you may have read, I found Nancy Reagan to be personally charming. After that comment she had to be.

Another time I was selected as one of forty recipients of the Golden Plate Award, a prestigious honor that has been given annually since 1961 to individuals who are recognized as "captains of achievement" in their respective fields. Not only did you receive an award, but as a role model you also got to meet 350 of the nation's best youth. They were fresh-faced and energetic, bright and highly talented. I got my inspiration from them, not the other way around.

I received my award along with Olympic gymnast Mary Lou Retton, Betty Ford, Ed Asner, Lionel Ritchie, T. Boone Pickens, and Elizabeth Taylor, among others. We were seated alphabetically. I sat next to Elizabeth Taylor. At one point in the evening, two brothers had each won respectively the math and science awards. While the awards program was supposed to be for teenagers only, these two were nine and eleven years of age. They pulled out a pair of violins and started playing an original composition. The older one explained that his younger brother had composed it two years earlier. Elizabeth Taylor and I looked at each other, gasping. She put a jeweled hand to her forehead and gripped it with despair. "What am I doing here!" she moaned. "This is talent!" Her eyes swept across the room.

"I know why you're here," I countered. "You can at least act. I don't have a clue as to why I'm here!" That was true. I was frankly very humbled to be at this gathering and in this company.

We both burst out laughing. I liked her very much. She was very down-to-earth and genuine, but kept staring at a thick packet of notes next to her plate. Each of the award recipients had been required to speak briefly at the dinner. Taylor was studying her notes as if she were memorizing an Academy Award acceptance speech. When she did get up to speak, she looked around the hall, put her face low to the microphone and murmured, "Thank you." Then she walked back to her chair.

"What happened?" I asked.

"I stood up there and looked at all those young faces and couldn't remember a thing." She drained a glass of water. "You know," she continued, "I wish you lived in California. We'd be great friends."

"Oh, sure," I said. "You with seven husbands and me the ex-nun."

25

OF THIEVES AND KINGS AND THEIR MONEY MACHINES

When I asked the other members of the board to reopen the hearings on the merger, there was a stunned silence. As one board member told a reporter later, "It was sort of a heavy thing."

Up until my administration, the attorney general hadn't played a very active role in the Board of Bank Incorporators. You sat *ex officio*. Other board members included a representative of the governor, the general treasurer, the director of the Department of Business Regulation, and a state senator. The board's job was to oversee any- and everything that pertained to banks, savings and loan associations, and credit unions, particularly applications for new charters and branch offices. Unfortunately for the depositors, it was a rubber-stamp board. If you wanted something, you got it. All you had to do was make a nice presentation and wait to receive the kiss of approval. It was nice and cozy.

I personally attended the regularly scheduled meetings of the board. The first time I walked in on one of those sessions, the cigars dropped out of a few mouths. They hadn't been expecting me. I don't believe they ever did get used to having me around.

We had a big problem almost immediately. The Bank of Boston had wanted to take over a Rhode Island bank, Rhode Island Hospital Trust. The Board of Bank Incorporators had already held hearings on the matter in 1984 and had approved the merger. But early in 1985, the Bank of Boston pleaded guilty to federal felony charges that it had failed to report the transfer of $1.2 billion through some Swiss banks. The federal government fined it a record $500,000. The bank chairman also admitted that it was possible that organized crime might have laundered as much as $2 million. Federal investigators had revealed that the money was brought to tellers in brown paper bags. I was opposed to any merger with RIHT until the Bank of Boston had cleared up some questions. When I asked the other members of the board to reopen the hearings on the merger, there was a stunned silence. As one board member told a reporter later, "It was sort of a heavy thing."

The board finally agreed to reopen the hearings. But the bank delayed in responding; it appeared it wouldn't. I went ahead with plans to intervene in a lawsuit filed by an RIHT stockholder to stop the merger. I wasn't interested in transporting organized-crime problems to Rhode Island.

Suddenly the bank decided it wanted to cooperate and make itself available for questioning. Bank representatives came before the board. Not because they wanted to, but because they had to. The hearing room was not very large. It looked like an unused schoolroom. Board members sat on an old-fashioned dais. Respondents sat before the board members at tables. The Boston people shuffled their papers importantly and appeared irritated.

As soon as everyone was ready, I asked the bank people, "What safeguards do you have in place so that you don't have these kinds of money-laundering problems again?"

"That is secret information," they replied.

I tried again. "How can we be sure that what happened to your bank won't happen to Rhode Island Hospital Trust, once it is taken over by you?"

"It won't happen again, but if you're asking about specifics, that's confidential information." They looked at each other with satisfaction.

"You've been aware of this problem for at least two years. You're familiar with the federal grand jury investigation that looked into these matters, and yet you elected not to tell the bank board about it when the original merger hearings took place. Why?" None of the other board members asked questions.

"We didn't disclose that information because it was part of a grand jury investigation and the federal government asked us not to talk about it."

I persisted. "But the grand jury was over with before the hearings on the merger took place, isn't that right?"

They slammed shut their briefcases and glared at me. Some of the board members said they had been satisfied with the testimony. I wasn't. I wanted the bank's full report on its internal management procedures, as well as a report on its own investigation. The bank promised to produce them promptly.

It took months of arm-twisting to get them. After careful consideration the board did approve the merger. But board members were furious with me. I had put their feet to the fire and upset the way business was done.

If I thought I could win them all, I was wrong. A local bank came knocking on our door seeking approval of a $3.5 million debenture. A former Democratic leader in the state legislature, whose family owned 40 percent of the bank, had made the pitch to the board. He had expected to get the go-ahead right away. He was politically well connected and a source of generous campaign contributions. The other board members saw no problem and had been ready to agree. But if you looked thoroughly at the assets of the institution and its financial history, it was questionable whether its assets could adequately cover the bond. This was no debenture he had been seeking; it was bail-out money from the depositors' pockets, and I was against it. This was the same bank that earlier the Department of Business Regulation had failed to examine, even though it is required by law to do so.

The failure to examine the bank had been disclosed only after the bank confirmed that it was under investigation by a federal grand jury. The federal authorities had been tracking possible currency violations similar to the Bank of Boston's. When asked about this by reporters, the director of DBR said, "I don't think this concerns us."

Apparently it didn't. I was outvoted 4 to 1.

PUBLIC CORRUPTION has an odor. But as one would to a landfill reeking with noxious fumes, after a while you get so used to the smell you don't notice it any longer. Maybe that's why the Rhode Island Housing and Mortgage Finance Corporation scandal continued for as long as it did.

RIHMFC, as it is called, is a quasipublic state government agency that has been around for years. It was supposed to provide low-interest mortgage money to low- and moderate-income people. The idea was to sell tax-exempt bonds in order to generate the money for these low-cost mortgage programs. RIHMFC's purpose was decent, to help people afford the American dream. But its practice wasn't. Deals were cut and money was made, but not for the people who needed it. The people who benefited were the people who put the money deals together, including the bank that serviced the accounts, the bond counsel and lawyer who wrote the bond programs, and their "special" friends who got cheap mortgages. When the RIHMFC investigation got under way, other states began investigations of their own publicly financed mortgage programs. They followed our lead.

I had always been interested in RIHMFC and Section 8 housing ever since a newspaper probe years earlier had turned up questions of wrongdoing: bribes, kickbacks, and rigged contract awards. They pointed to politics and collusion. My predecessor had been forced to bring the allegations to a grand jury. The grand jury came back empty-handed. Roberts said there were nineteen witnesses he hadn't been able to contact; that's why the investigation had come to a halt. I didn't believe it, and neither did a lot of other people. It became a campaign issue in 1982 and in 1984.

In my speeches around the state I had talked about auditing records at state agencies to make sure that taxpayers' money was being spent correctly. Two agencies in particular had stood out: the Department of Transportation, and RIHMFC. During the 1984 campaign I had spotted some irregularities in bidding practices at D.O.T. and had called for an investigation. Roberts looked at the allegations superficially. Then I was elected and we began an investigation in earnest.

One of my investigators said, "I think you should examine what appears to be an interesting pattern." We pored over documents. He pointed to various names and flipped pages. "Look here, and here," he said, "and here. The same names keep appearing. It seems that only certain people are getting the nod for contracts. Others are being shut out." Our RIHMFC investigation turned up a similar pattern of coziness. Both investigations revealed that a certain "club" of individuals appeared to control business in the state. If you didn't belong, you didn't play.

Around this time the local newspaper reported that two politicians had received questionable RIHMFC mortgages. I wondered who else might have them. I decided to expand our

Section 8 probe of RIHMFC to include single-family mortgages. I asked to see RIHMFC's records. But the executive director of RIHMFC had allegedly ordered the shredding of all the records and erasure of the computer files. Word had already reached the street that we had targeted RIHMFC.

I called the state police and it stood guard over whatever records we could salvage. Then we got lucky. An investigator in our office figured out how to bring back RIHMFC's computer memory. He pressed some buttons and we were able to re-create the erased files. We looked at each other in disbelief. Somebody started yelling and we began pounding each other on the back. Pretty soon we were all shouting and jumping up and down. The floor shook. People on the floor below thought somebody was dancing on their ceiling.

Investigating white-collar crime is like trying to follow an unfamiliar road map. There are many twists and turns and dead ends. Gone are the days of simply checking a bank account and finding a mysterious $50,000 deposit. That payoff was easy to spot. Nowadays you have to be an expert in practically every financial venture you can think of, and born with a hunting dog's instincts. If the payoff is $25,000, somebody may sell the person you are investigating a $100,000 house for $75,000. You have to be able to sniff that out. Or that individual may be given a bearer bond, which doesn't require a name on it. It just says, "Pay to bearer." All your target has to do is hold the bond, then cash it when the crime for which he or she is being investigated is too old to prosecute.

We looked for patterns. Finding them proved to be easier than making the connections. But we had begun peeling the onion, and with each layer we uncovered, there was always one more.

We divided the investigation into five teams. Each team had a lawyer who acted as a consultant, an investigator, a state policeman, an auditor, and a local cop. They helped one another and acted as checks on each other. We met nightly as a group to discuss our progress and problems. The group meetings continued throughout my two years in office.

After hearing testimony and reviewing evidence, the investigative grand jury returned indictments. Among those charged with crimes—ranging from obstruction of justice, and filing false documents, to obtaining mortgages to which they were not entitled—were the executive director of RIHMFC, other RIHMFC employees, a former speaker of the house, the governor's top aide, the governor's state police driver, Fleet National Bank (the entity), and some of Fleet's high-ranking officers.

Political favoritism is not a crime in Rhode Island, but the executive director of RIHMFC had also given preferable mortgages to sons and daughters and relatives of politicians and powerful people. It pointed to the very problem we were trying to rub out, special interests that received special treatment. Many people who really qualified for low-interest mortgages didn't get them. The money had already been used up. When we subpoenaed the personal records of the executive director, we found that even though he earned under $100,000 a year from his RIHMFC salary, he had amassed $23 million in assets. In addition to criminal charges against him, we also filed a civil suit for treble damages.

When you looked at the components and then at the whole of the RIHMFC scandal, there had been no competition in any of the bid procedures. And there wasn't meant to be. The people who had created the mortgage program and got it passed in the legislature were the same ones who serviced it. The fees that the bond underwriter got, for example, were astronomical compared to what competitive underwriters received elsewhere in the country. This was a practice that had gone on for years unchallenged. It appeared to be a grand self-enrichment scheme, the stocking of personal fiefs as if they were exotic aquariums, and RIHMFC had footed the bill.

But the conflict of interest didn't stop at RIHMFC. The coziness spread like honey on warm bread to other agencies and authorities. We saw a collective of names over and over again, the same people sitting on several boards, or members of their management, helping themselves to thick slices of the public loaf. Unlike state agencies, these quasipublic entities wrote their own laws, ensuring their own success. Nothing ever had to go to bid, and didn't. The members of these boards didn't vote on their own companies to perform the work on publicly financed projects. They voted on each other's. It was clear that the people who ran the state, those with the most to gain, wanted to keep it that way.

RIHMFC, which already occupied some pretty plush offices, had signed a contract to move into new quarters at the Fleet Center, owned by Fleet National Bank. I asked for a copy of the contract. We noticed that Fleet Bank would not only snare a substantial tenant, but was also provided very generous terms in its lease agreement. RIHMFC would have to pay the bank millions of dollars over the lifetime of the contract, costing Rhode Island taxpayers a fortune.

One of my investigators piped up. "What a joke," he said. "For the money you'd think you'd get gold filigree on the walls. About the only thing you do get *is* the walls. The office space is nothing but a shell. It comes to a floor, ceiling, and walls. You provide everything else. It's the most expensively leased unit of all the offices available."

"Who built the Fleet Center?" I asked.

"Gilbane," voices blended in chorus. "They are partners in this venture." The Gilbane Building Corporation had figured prominently in an unrelated investigation conducted jointly by my office and the federal government. We brought the company to trial. In addition, the administrative head of Gilbane sits on the board of some of those authorities I have mentioned earlier that voted on each other's interests.

I publicly questioned the lease and advised the governor how to get out of it. We didn't think it was in the best interests of the people. Fleet Bank said the lease stood, then later backed down, reluctantly, and with anger. I had upended the financial kingpins. On their Monopoly board of wheeling and dealing, I had passed Go and won Boardwalk. I had also won another distinction: Fleet Bank publicly accused me of being on a "witch-hunt."

Without any competitive bidding, the State Public Building Authority gave Gilbane a contract to construct a state office building. The company said it could do it for $11 million. When the Building Authority decided that it wanted a parking garage to go with the building, Gilbane again got the contract without bid. The total cost jumped to $42 million. I publicly questioned the practice of closed bids, but the Building Authority didn't blink an eye. The contract went through.

I had taken on well-respected members of the community. Their equals, the opinion leaders in Rhode Island, judges and journalists, were stunned. I remember a conversation I had with an editorial writer of the Providence *Journal-Bulletin.* We had been discussing public information about a construction company under indictment for falsifying documents. It had allegedly set up a phony minority front in order to qualify for government construction jobs. The veteran journalist said, "Why are you going after those guys? It's just part of the business of getting government contracts. Everybody does it. I don't see any crime there. The crime is with the government."

My spine turned to ice. If the people who reported the news didn't think there had been a crime, what chance did the public have of understanding that there was? The people's views are shaped by what they read, see, and hear.

"We have laws that say it's a crime whether you agree or disagree," I said. The newsman just looked at me. "Do you mean to tell me," I pressed, "that unless there is a gun and a dead body, you would say there was no crime? You accept murder as a crime because it's vicious and graphic. You're used to that. You don't accept white-collar crime or public corruption because it's not." The chill had extended down my arms. I turned to leave. "Remember, you can steal money just as easily with a pencil as you can with a gun." I winked. "They're both against the law."

Not only was the attitude toward white-collar crime difficult to change, it was also very hard to present the details of such crimes to a jury. No matter how simple you tried to make it, most people just weren't able to grasp the complexity of numbers and what they were supposed to mean. They weren't financial experts and the material was deadly enough to put you to sleep. As a matter of fact, in a few of the cases we brought to trial, some jurors *did* fall asleep. One of the first juries in this kind of case acquitted Ralph Pari and a Fleet bank officer of felony charges.

Juries basically tried to do the best they could. While we convicted the governor's top aide on one charge in our first RIHMFC trial, the jury found him not guilty on the other, more serious charge. The judge, a no-nonsense jurist, was shocked. In open court he said that had he been making the determination, he would have found the defendant guilty. We had asked for jail, but the judge didn't impose it. That established the benchmark for the other judges to follow. We had also wanted jail in the remaining cases, but never got it.

I had spoken so often about seeking jail sentences in public corruption cases that when it didn't happen in the RIHMFC trials, it was as if I had gone back on my word. Particularly when one of the cases we turned over to the U.S. Attorney for prosecution resulted in a prison term. The record of federal judges is tougher than that of state court judges. Their courts aren't clogged like most state courts throughout the land. In addition, federal prosecutors can pick and choose their cases, usually the winners. State prosecutors can't. Unless the case is virtually unprosecutable, you have to proceed, or stand accused yourself of burying cases. I felt the public compared the two systems and concluded that we hadn't done our job.

Right before the November 1986 election, another judge reopened the aide's case on the basis of alleged prosecutorial misconduct. The news electrified the public and cast a broad and brooding shadow over the office and its prosecutors. Defense lawyer John Sheehan represented the governor's top aide. He was an old friend of Judge DeRobbio and often called the judge publicly by his boyhood name, "Zeke." Sheehan wanted his good friend to reexamine his client's case. He claimed that the prosecution had withheld information pertinent to his client. The information to which Sheehan referred concerned a separate investigation, and had nothing to do with the charges brought against the defendant. Judge DeRobbio, who has acknowledged that at the same time he had also been approached by the governor to seek the appointment of chief of District Court, agreed to meet privately with Sheehan to discuss the case. No prosecutor was present. The case was reopened, and the governor appointed Judge DeRobbio his new chief of District Court. Following my departure from office, the governor's aide was retried, this time before a judge, not a jury. The judge found him not guilty. In explaining his decision the judge stated that the aide didn't understand the documents he signed or their legal significance. The aide, an astute veteran politician, was studying for his doctor of laws degree at the time he signed the documents.

WE BROUGHT a number of RIHMFC cases. Almost all of them ended with the defendants pleading to the charges. But I had to request the court several times to expedite the two main cases that represented the thrust of our public corruption efforts. Instead, the court kept putting the smaller cases first.

Our biggest and oldest RIHMFC cases didn't even get scheduled on the calendar although there was a public urgency to their being heard: People deserved to know the facts behind public corruption. The Gilbane case, by contrast, got tried almost immediately. The company said there had been a compelling public interest to clear its name. The judges hastened the case through.

After a while the public began to lose interest in RIHMFC. Former front-page stories ended up on the back page. The spotlight on public corruption had faded and with it any chance the people had of cleaning up their state. That was a very lonely moment for me. I had wanted the people to keep heart.

I was a frequent dinner speaker and I used those occasions to bolster the fight against public corruption. "Conflict of interest is corruption, too," I said. "Every time you act out of your interests and not the people's, you are abusing the public trust." But I don't think most people really cared. When my 1986 opponent for reelection, who remains an RIHMFC bondholder, accepted campaign contributions from the bosses and ranking members of companies under state indictment, or publicly known to be under investigation, companies that he would have to prosecute if he were elected attorney general, the public shrugged its shoulders.

(Under my successor, the RIHMFC investigation came to a sliding halt. Eight months after taking office, no new investigations were begun or old ones finished. The Providence *Journal-Bulletin* in an August 1987 editorial complained that Attorney General O'Neil had also failed to bring RIHMFC cases to trial. Any momentum against public corruption that my administration had tried to accelerate had clearly peaked.

(On a defense motion to drop charges in August 1987, Superior Court Judge John Orton dismissed conspiracy and obstruction of the judicial system counts against Ralph Pari and a big-name politician, former Speaker of the Rhode Island House, Edward P. Manning. In dismissing the counts Judge Orton said that while there was no doubt that the books had been cooked, no grand jury had been sitting at the time records had been altered or shredded. This, of course, is not only preposterous, it misses the point. Under Rhode Island law, the obstruction of the judicial system statute is drawn deliberately broad to allow for the inclusion of such crimes, i.e., deliberately destroying incriminating material and re-creating new records for their ultimate submission to a grand jury.

(Cleaning up public corruption is no easy task, particularly when years and years of abuse in office have numbed the minds of the public to unacceptable levels of tolerance. Until the public is behind efforts to eliminate corruption, cases will get thrown out and juries will return not guilty verdicts.)

Just before the election Judge Domenic Cresto threw out one of our RIHMFC cases on grounds of prosecutorial misconduct. It was a significant case. My staff and I were speechless. There had been absolutely no legal precedent for his decision. In addition, instead of relying on the entire transcript of testimony when he made his ruling, he had referred to only a few pages. We appealed his decision, but the ruling seemed calculated to strike a deathblow. I think it must have worked. The public was agitated.

Allegations of prosecutorial misconduct never came up in the beginning or middle of my administration. Only at the end.

During the height of the RIHMFC investigation, Governor Edward DiPrete had announced that he was going to institute bid procedures at all quasipublic agencies like RIHMFC in order to open up the process. It was part of a housecleaning that was supposed to restore public confidence. But later he designed and tried to push through legislation that provided for one big, super agency that not only eliminated the need to go before the other little quasipublic agencies, but also closed forever the door on accountability. This new "super board" didn't have to follow bid procedures and couldn't be court-challenged. The governor said it was part of an economic reform package.

I raised a howl of protest. The governor became very angry and reluctantly withdrew the bill.

We had learned nothing.

26
CONFLICTS

"By your own account, Henry, you have jeopardized the public trust. People expect, and rightfully so, that prosecutors should stay at arm's length from people they're going to prosecute."

Joseph Voccola was president of the Johnston town council. He also rolled back odometers on used cars. He was pretty good at it until the law caught up with him. He pleaded guilty to three counts of odometer tampering and was sentenced to a year in federal prison in Pennsylvania. On the way out the door, he announced that he planned to remain an active council member while in prison and phone in his votes.

Rhode Island had earned yet another black eye. Who would believe that a convicted felon would be allowed to keep his seat and conduct official public business from prison? But most of the people who lived in Johnston did. They supported Voccola, even though it meant that none of his voting could be done publicly as required by law.

My office filed action in the Rhode Island Supreme Court to stop Voccola. We lost, but it had given us an opportunity to raise the issue of public accountability and conduct. The attitude of the people had been just as disturbing as Voccola's. Public corruption cannot flourish unless it is tolerated.

Which brings me to Henry Gemma, the former chief of my criminal division, the man who helped retry Von Bülow, and the man I fired over an issue of professional ethics.

Henry was a career prosecutor with fourteen years under his

belt working for several attorneys general. While Henry was employed by my predecessor, he took a vacation in Florida the month before I took office, and ended up visiting a man down there who was under state indictment by a Rhode Island grand jury.

Late in the first year of my term, U.S. Attorney Lincoln Almond called to inform me that somebody had fingered Henry for soliciting a bribe.

"What are the circumstances?" I asked.

Almond replied, "Joe DiSanto claims Henry wanted fifty thousand dollars to drop his case." DiSanto was a former Providence Public Works official who had been indicted in a kickback scheme. He was the man Henry had visited in Florida. "He came in with Buddy Cianci." Cianci was a former mayor of Providence and a lawyer, who had lost office over an assault-and-battery charge.

I agreed with Almond that he should investigate the charges.

Early the next morning, Henry, who had been informed by John Sheehan that he was the subject of an investigation, asked to see me. He had brought Sheehan with him. He told me that the defense lawyer was representing him in the Almond investigation. I was surprised. The attorney general's office prosecuted Sheehan's clients and Henry would have to be Sheehan's adversary on those cases.

I asked Henry to put Sheehan in the conference room and for Henry to come into my office alone. He was agitated. His cheeks were bright with color.

"Boss, John Sheehan called me and asked me to come over to see him. To tell you the truth, I thought he had some information that some organized-crime guys were going to rub me out. It wasn't that at all. Instead, he told me that some people are saying that I solicited a bribe. I want to tell you, right here and now, I did not solicit any bribe."

"Henry, I'm in somewhat of an uncomfortable position. I just want to caution you that anything you say might be used against you if I get called in as a witness." I had just "mirandized" our conversation.

But Henry persisted. "Boss, I have nothing to hide and I want to tell you everything that happened." He cleared his throat and began. "I drove down to Florida with my girl friend, Susan, and Bill, a lawyer friend of mine. We had gone for the week. Bill kept trying to get me to go over to see Joe DiSanto. But I said no. One day Bill asked me to pick him up at DiSanto's. I said that would be all right, but be out in front. He was nowhere in sight when Susan and I drove up. I didn't want to send Susan up the steps to ring the doorbell because I didn't know the neighborhood, so I went. DiSanto answered the door. He invited Susan and me in and said, 'I hear from Bill that you're looking for a condo. I have a three-bedroom across the way for sale. I'll give you a tour of this two-bedroom, which is similar, while you're waiting for Bill.' While I was there, the phone rang. DiSanto answered it and said that there was a friend of mine on the other end. It turned out to be John Hawkins." Hawkins was a former state senator, who is legal counsel to the Rhode Island lottery. "I spoke to him for about five minutes. Then DiSanto asked if I wanted to see his other condo."

"Did you go to see it?"

"Yes I did, Boss."

"What happened then?"

"Well, we left the first building and walked across a parking lot and went into the unit. He told me he was selling it for sixty-one thousand dollars. I really didn't want a three-bedroom, so I told him I wasn't interested."

I couldn't believe what the chief of my criminal division had told me. But he looked at me expectantly, as if he should have been rewarded for his candor.

"Henry, were you in the market for a condominium in Florida?"

Henry nodded.

"Of all the places you could have looked, why did you look at a condominium for sale by a man you had under indictment? A man whose case you virtually control as chief of the criminal division? If he had it tagged for sixty-one thousand dollars, but sold it to you for sixty thousand dollars, it would be logical for people to conclude that you might have taken a thousand-dollar kickback. What on earth were you thinking of?"

But Henry remained firm. "Boss, I did nothing wrong."

"By your own account, Henry, you have jeopardized the public trust. People expect, and rightfully so, that prosecutors should stay at arm's length from people they're going to prosecute. What kind of a message do you think this sends people? All you had to do was ring the doorbell, say, 'Hello, Joe. Tell Bill I'm waiting for him in the car,' and turn around and walk back down the steps. But not you."

Blotches of anger spotted Henry's face. He pulled himself stiffly back into his chair.

I tried to look at it from his point of view of ringing the bell and being polite and a prosecutor at the same time. "Look, Henry. I could even see you going in and trying to be courteous, and trying to get out of there fast because of the public perception that kind of encounter lends itself to. I don't like that, but I could see something like that happening. And I would say, 'All right, Henry, you made a mistake going in, but you tried to get out of there fast.' Instead, you sit here in front of me, tell me that you're looking to buy a condo, not only do you go into DiSanto's, but you also take a tour, accept a five-minute phone call, walk across a parking lot to look at another condo with DiSanto, discuss the sale price, and then leave. That is not what you call a quick departure. The public would have a right to question what you were doing there."

Henry said tersely, "Well, Boss, I told Dennis Roberts about this when I got back from Florida and he just laughed."

"Henry, I want to think about this. Come back and see me this afternoon."

When I saw Henry that afternoon, I asked him if he thought there was any way that he had undermined the public confidence in the attorney general's office and, the larger question, in the criminal justice system. Or if, at a minimum, his conduct constituted an appearance of impropriety. He said he didn't think so.

Henry's conduct, as reported to me in his own words, crystallizes the problem of public corruption in Rhode Island. Rhode Islanders know that ethical standards exist, but they never demand that they be put in place, lived up to, or made a part of their lives.

Henry had been looked up to by the prosecutors, and was a longtime favorite with the community and the media. But he had been unable to show any insight that his conduct had compromised the integrity of his public responsibilities. I had talked about violation of the public trust where it concerned others; for the first time that I was aware of, it concerned my own office. I owed the public and the prosecutors the best they deserved. To have done nothing about Henry would have sent wrong signals to both, and what I had been trying to build during my administration would have come tumbling down.

I placed Henry on leave to give him some time to think things over. I spoke with him by phone. He repeated that he had done "nothing wrong," and refused to see that his conduct had created an appearance of impropriety, damaging his public trust. Reluctantly, I fired him.

Henry asked me for due process. I brought the matter to the Disciplinary Counsel. That review board claimed to the media that full hearings had been held and that everybody had been heard from. Everybody apparently but me, the person who had brought the complaint. I was never summoned to testify.

The review board cleared Henry of any ethical questions.

* * *

I HAVE made legislative proposals to both the Disciplinary Counsel and the Commission on Judicial Tenure and Discipline to open up the review process once probable cause is established, and make it more accountable to the people. Behind the scenes certain judges have supported modified legislation, which ensures the continued secrecy of the process, prevents any public record of the proceedings, and protects the identity of those judges whose actions are reviewed. The only time the public gets to hear about the review process is when the chairman of the commission thinks the public needs to. At the time of the consideration of the legislation I was out of office, but on a radio talk show I host five nights a week on WKRI I asked the audience to demand an open process. The public howled and these judges retreated. The process opened up.

27
BUILDING BUDDIES

I knew instinctively that I had lost my bid for reelection.

Henry's dismissal occurred at the end of my first year in office. The dismissal of the Gilbane construction company case occurred toward the end of my second. Conduct in office was at the heart of both.

The office of attorney general together with the U.S. Department of Transportation had investigated the Gilbane company for allegedly setting up a minority front to gain government contracts. Federal law required that 10 percent of the work on federal construction projects be performed by a minority-owned company. No minority contractor, no award. We had charged that Gilbane used a minority contractor to make it look as if the contractor had done the work, when in reality Gilbane had hired a nonminority contractor to do it. Gilbane got the job; the minority contractor allegedly got a payment in return. We proceeded against Gilbane, but Gilbane also proceeded against us. The company's lawyers went to several different Superior Court judges to get the criminal charges against their client thrown out. Each time the courts rebuffed them. Then the company filed a $5 million civil suit against me in federal court. The judge hearing the matter refused to go forward with it, saying the company had tried to have the federal court interfere with the pending criminal case. The federal court judge stated that Gilbane had brought the civil suit "diabolically."

The administrative head of the company, Paul Choquette, personally crusaded in the media to drum me out of office. He said over and over, "I have a missionary zeal" to remove Violet. When my 1986 opponent for reelection, Jim O'Neil, announced his candidacy for office, Choquette held a major fund-raiser for him. O'Neil said he had accepted Choquette's support and money "proudly." O'Neil also accepted help in his election efforts from Fleet Bank, under state indictment, and a number of its high-ranking officers. On election night O'Neil even went to the home of the bank's president and chief executive officer to celebrate his apparent victory.

THE GILBANE case had suddenly appeared on the trial calendar. Judge Joseph Rodgers was assigned to it. The judge belonged to the same exclusive country club of 365 members, which included some of the Gilbane family. We believed that constituted an appearance of a conflict of interest. I asked Rodgers to step down from the case. A hearing on the issue was held. Rodgers presided over it, swearing himself in, then testified and ruled favorably on the credibility of his own statements, saying that it was okay for him to act as trial judge. Gilbane had waived a jury trial. I was very worried: Rodgers was the sole fact-finder in the case; he would decide it. We appealed to the Rhode Island Supreme Court. It ruled against us, allowing Rodgers to hear the case. None of the Supreme Court judges signed the opinion, which stated that the training of judges made them superior to ordinary people. Unlike jurors, they could transcend the prejudices of ordinary people. A member of the jury who knew a defendant still had to be eliminated from a trial proceeding. But before the trial started, Rodgers decided to step down. He said there had been too much "negative publicity" surrounding the case.

This was not the first time Judge Rodgers and I had had a confrontation. When Judge Bevilacqua resigned, a slot had opened up on the Supreme Court. Many jurists, including Rodgers, had applied for it. But the state's chief organized-crime lawyer, John Cicilline, had complained in an affidavit that Rodgers had reneged on an agreement he had made with one of Cicilline's clients. Cicilline stated that the judge had coached him *ex parte* on how to get a sentence reduced for an organized-crime figure, who had to appear before Rodgers and two other judges reviewing the matter. Cicilline said Rodgers had advised him to waive his client's rights. In return, Rodgers would see to it that his client's sentence was reduced. After the convict had waived the rights, the panel voted not to reduce his sentence.

While I was elated that this organized-crime figure didn't have his sentence reduced, I was concerned about alleged *ex parte* coaching by a judge who had applied for the top judge's job in Rhode Island. I asked the state police to investigate. It was responsible for all the background checks on the Supreme Court candidates. An investigation also provided the candidate a chance to tell his or her side of the story. The state police reported to me that the key legislators sitting on the panel processing the candidates had made an agreement with Rodgers geared to avoid any embarrassment. The judge would withdraw his name from consideration; the panel would pronounce him a fit candidate. The judge would then announce that he was no longer interested in the position.

The Cicilline affidavit had been filed before the Rhode Island Supreme Court, where five judges sit. The state police had also discussed the affidavit with Rodgers' boss, Judge Giannini. I asked the state police if the judges were going to proceed with a complaint to the Commission on Judicial Tenure and Discipline, headed by Rodgers, to find out whether there was any merit to the charges.

"No."

"Not even Judge Giannini, the presiding judge?"

"No."

JUDGE CRESTO, who had thrown out a key RIHMFC case weeks earlier, even though there had been no legal precedent on which to base his decision, was assigned to the Gilbane trial. Like Rodgers before him, he was the sole arbiter of guilt or innocence. My heart sank like a block of concrete falling to the ocean floor.

The trial had been scheduled just days before the election. But during the discovery phase, the prosecutor in the case had failed to turn over to the defense the full transcript of a tape-recorded interview with a key witness. He had given only a synopsis of it. I learned about this after the court session at which the defense had brought it to the attention of the judge. The prosecutor said it had been an oversight and was "no big problem." I disagreed. It went right to the heart of fair play. It was the basic ingredient of integrity. A key belief and major focus was on the line: propriety in office.

I met with some of the legal staff the following morning to discuss points of law about the case. You couldn't deny the fact that the prosecution had played unfairly. I felt I had no option but to dismiss the case: It was the right thing to do.

Gilbane never got its day in court. Under the rules of double jeopardy, the company cannot be tried again for the same alleged offenses.

Judge Cresto had emphasized publicly that he was going to hold a full hearing on the withholding of evidence to the defense. I welcomed the hearing. I had directed the prosecutors not to dismiss the case until after the judge's hearing. But the judge changed his mind. He said our decision to dismiss took the case out of his hands. But we had not filed any formal action dismissing the case, and had made it plain in open court that we wanted the hearing. Instead, the judge called for a special prosecutor to investigate the office of attorney general.

During my predecessor's administration the Rhode Island Supreme Court had found more than a half-dozen cases of prosecutorial misconduct. Yet nobody had called for a special prosecutor to investigate his office. Just my office, and, at that, only allegations of prosecutorial misconduct.

I SAT in my office, alone. The dismissal of the Gilbane case had occurred four days before the election, but events surrounding the Gilbane trial had escalated rapidly. I knew instinctively that I had lost my bid for reelection. The public couldn't withstand the specter of a court-appointed special prosecutor hanging over the office. Confidence in my administration was bound to hit bottom. I stared out the windows. Dusk had come early. It had been a unique opportunity to restore a faded dream.

I had already been conducting my own in-house investigation of the Gilbane events through the internal affairs unit. I turned over its findings to the state police for its review. But the court wasn't satisfied. The judges appointed a special prosecutor. I hired a Washington law firm to protect the constitutional interests of the office. The constitutional rights of all future Rhode Island attorneys general could be jeopardized. I refused to allow another branch of government, the judiciary, to intimidate the office. A special prosecutor meant that anytime a judge didn't like what cases you were prosecuting, or issues over which you had challenged a judge, all the judge had to do to stop them was whisper "prosecutorial misconduct," and institute a hearing.

Before my term in office had been completed, the judges

backed down and called off the special prosecutor. They said my political opponent, and newly elected attorney general, Jim O'Neil, had agreed to review allegations of prosecutorial misconduct.

After having promised to complete and make public his report of the inquiry by the end of March 1987, O'Neil finally finished it in August and declared that it was up to Judge Giannini to release to the public the report. Judge Giannini stated it was up to O'Neil, not him.

The report was eventually made public in September. It essentially corroborated my own internal investigation with a finding that I had no direct or indirect involvement in any wrongdoing of the prosecutor.

EPILOGUE

Two years is not a very long time to try to turn around entrenched habits and public attitudes. As a matter of fact, it's downright impossible. But for me, doing the impossible is a challenge, not an obstacle.

When I was a young nun, I did some independent reading on comparative religions. I was particularly interested in Buddhism. A master was teaching his students. "Once there was a young man," he said, "who was walking in the jungle. It was a beautiful sunlit day. His heart sparkled with joy. Suddenly, the hairs on the back of his neck prickled in fear. He heard the roar of a lion close behind him. He didn't turn around; he ran as fast as he could. The animal's hot breath scorched his back. Soon he came to the edge of a cliff. He had no choice. He dropped over the side and began to inch his way downward. He was about midway when he heard the chilling growl of another lion, only this time below him. He was weary and his hands were sweaty. They began to slip. Immediately to his left he saw a clump of green, and in the middle the most beautiful flower he had ever seen. He could save his life if he just grabbed it. Instead, he touched it delicately, brushing his fingers against the moist petals, and fell to the waiting abyss below."

When I first read that story, I thought to myself, What a fool!

Now that I am older, I respect the wisdom of that Buddhist

monk. He taught his students a valuable lesson. That lesson has blossomed into others. I have determined that in my life I don't want to grab at it in order to be a full human being. I want to leave behind for others something beautiful, and know that it was the last thing that I touched.